Tempting Traditions with Worthy Additions

By
Marie Louise Everson Smart

PublishAmerica
Baltimore

© 2004 by Marie Louise Everson Smart.
All rights reserved. No part of this book may be reproduced, stored in a retrieval system or transmitted in any form or by any means without the prior written permission of the publishers, except by a reviewer who may quote brief passages in a review to be printed in a newspaper, magazine or journal.

First printing

ISBN: 1-4137-1404-8
PUBLISHED BY PUBLISHAMERICA, LLLP
www.publishamerica.com
Baltimore

Printed in the United States of America

DEDICATION

Several years ago, when my children, John and Jean, were early teenagers, they asked if I would write down all the family recipes they had enjoyed through the years. I rather liked that idea and so this book was born. It is to them and their father, my husband Jack, that I dedicate with all my love *Tempting Traditions With Worthy Additions.*

Acknowledgements

This book of our family's culinary treasures would not be possible without the generosity of good friends and relatives. Without them I would not have been able to compile these recipes. I did not invent them. All I did was collect and use them over the years. To all who contributed to this volume, my sincere thanks.

And special gratitude to my daughter, Jean Marie. It was she who encouraged me to write. It was she who designed the layout. It was she who drew the charming illustrations and it was she who named the book.

Tempting Traditions with Worthy Additions

By
Marie Louise Everson Smart

HORS D'OEUVRES

I REMEMBER . . . the days when we offered our guests an assortment of before-dinner snacks. More often than not, today's guests seem to decline when offered appetizers. As a result, we spend less time than we used to on that part of the menu and serve simply a delicious cheese or a few specialty nuts before the main course. Nonetheless, it is good to have a few favorite and distinctive recipes that can be offered on special occasions.

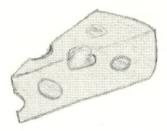

A JOHN ROOT CREATION
Yield: 24 - 36 rounds

John Root! I need not say more! John was our good neighbor in Solebury and a magnificent cook!

½ pound **cream cheese**
a little **light cream**
1 teaspoon **dry mustard**
1 teaspoon **Worcestershire sauce**
1 tablespoon **dry bread crumbs**
1 loaf of **thinly sliced white bread**
small **sweet onions**, sliced
Parmesan cheese, grated

Soften the cream cheese, using a little light cream. Add the Worcestershire sauce, dry mustard and bread crumbs. Cut rounds of bread and toast. Put a thinly sliced onion round on each round of bread. Cover with cream cheese and roll in Parmesan cheese. Broil until lightly brown and bubbly.

CHICKEN WONTONS
Yield: approximately 36

Jeannie made these for us for our Christmas Midnight Supper in 1992. We've enjoyed this special treat many, many times since then!

Wontons
8 ounces **breast of chicken**, diced
½ cup shredded **carrot**
¼ cup finely chopped **celery** or **water chestnuts**
1 tablespoon **soy sauce**
1 tablespoon **sherry**
2 teaspoons **cornstarch**
2 teaspoons grated **ginger-root**
wonton wrappers, which can be purchased in almost any super market.

Mix all the above, except the wrappers, of course! Spoon rounded teaspoon of filling onto wrapper. Brush edges with water, bringing opposite points together. Pinch and seal. Place on greased sheet and bake at 375 degrees for 8 to 10 minutes, until brown and crisp. Serve with sweet and sour sauce.

Sweet and Sour Sauce
2 cups granulated sugar
1 cup white vinegar
1 teaspoon salt
¼ cup grated carrots
¼ cup very finely minced red pepper

Combine the sugar, vinegar, and salt in a large saucepan. Simmer gently until it has been reduced to 1 ½ cups. Add the carrot and red pepper and cool to room temperature.

STUFFED CHERRY TOMATOES

Yield: Your Choice

These always were a colorful and tasty addition to our table of appetizers.

Cherry tomatoes, rinsed and patted dry.
Celery leaves and **chive sprigs** for decoration.

With a sharp knife, cut cap off tomatoes. With a small spoon remove seeds and turn tomatoes upside down onto paper towels to drain. With a small spoon pack the tomatoes in any of the following ways. Cover with caps, garnish with celery leaves and chive sprigs. Chill.

The following three stuffings were most popular, but with a little imagination you can dream up many other variations on this theme.

Stuffing One:
Place a **smoked oyster** or **mussel** in each tomato.
Cover with caps and garnish.

Stuffing Two:
3 ounces soft **blue cheese**
1/4 cup **cottage cheese**, small curd
2 tablespoons fresh chopped **chives**
freshly **ground pepper**.
Blend blue cheese with cottage cheese and chives until smooth. Add pepper. Fill tomatoes.

Stuffing Three:
2 cups tightly packed fresh **basil leaves OR**
1 cup **basil leaves** and 1 cup **fresh parsley**
1/2 cup **olive oil**
2 tablespoons **pine nuts** or **walnuts**
3 **garlic** cloves, chopped
salt and freshly **ground pepper**
1/2 cup freshly grated **Parmesan cheese**

Combine basil, oil, nuts, garlic, salt and pepper in blender and mix until smooth. Stir in Parmesan. Fill tomatoes.

NOTE: The pesto can be made several days ahead, covered and refrigerated.

ELEGANT ENDIVE BOATS
Yield: 12 -15 boats

One of the most "worthy additions."

1 **Belgian endive**
1/2 cup **Roquefort** or **Bleu Cheese**
1/2 cup **Philadelphia Cream Cheese**
1 large **red skinned apple**, sliced

Separate endive leaves and put in cold water to crisp. Blend the bleu cheese and cream cheese. When ready to serve, dry leaves and put a good dab of cheese on each leaf. Crown with a slice of unpeeled apple.

PICKLED SHRIMP
Yield: 26 - 30 count

These are delicious as is, impaled on toothpicks. Or if you prefer, you can use them as a filling for medium sized avocados, which have been halved and peeled.

1 pound raw **shrimp**
1/3 cup **white wine vinegar**
1/4 cup **olive oil**
1/2 cup dry **white table wine**
1 tablespoon each **salt**, **sugar** and **pickling spice**
1 small **onion**

Peel and de-vein the raw shrimp. Put them in a saucepan with the vinegar, olive oil, wine, salt, sugar, pickling spice and onion. Bring to a boil and simmer for 3 minutes – or just until the shrimp turn pink. Allow to cool in the liquid.

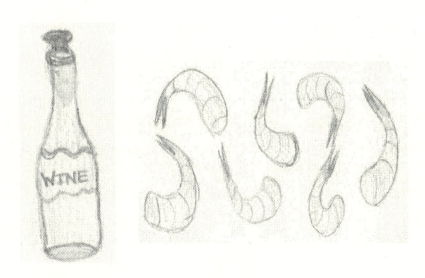

SCOTTISH SAUSAGE CRESCENTS
Yield: 24

This was really a favorite of the three "J's." It looks tedious and complicated, but once you've done it, it's a piece of cake. We served these at a couple of Christmas vestry parties and they were a hit. We had them, as well, at our own family midnight Christmas Eve buffet.

Hot Mustard Sauce
½ cup very hot **dry mustard**
½ cup **apple-cider vinegar**
½ cup **granulated sugar**
1 **egg yolk**

Makes 1 ½ cups.

Combine dry mustard and vinegar in a small bowl. Cover and allow to stand overnight. In the morning, in a small saucepan, combine mustard and vinegar mixture, sugar and egg yolk. Simmer over medium-low heat, stirring constantly, until slightly thickened

Sausage Crescents
1 package (10 ounces) **frozen patty shells**
1 pound hot **sausage meat**
1 **egg** beaten

Allow patty shells to defrost in refrigerator overnight, or on kitchen counter until workable, but always keep them cold to the touch. In a skillet saute sausage meat until browned and cooked through. Remove from heat and drain. Put sausage into a bowl and add the egg. Allow to cool.

To Assemble:

Stack 3 patty shells with edges aligned. Press together with heel of hand to flatten. Using a rolling pin, roll out to a 10 inch circle, trimming edges evenly, and cut into 8 triangles. Place about 1 tablespoon of filling on wide end of each triangle. Brush the tip of each triangle with water and roll into crescent and place tip down on an ungreased cookie sheet. Repeat procedure with remaining patty shells. At this point you may wrap and freeze or continue to next step. Preheat the oven to 400 degrees. Bake 15 minutes or until golden brown. Serve with hot mustard.

SOUFFLE CRACKERS
Yield: your choice

Presumably this was a "White House" specialty during the Kennedy administration. Jeannie made these many times – and always to perfection!

Melted **butter**
Ice **water**
Saltine crackers

Pre-heat oven to 400 degrees. Brush baking sheet with melted butter. Fill a shallow pan with ice water. Add crackers and let them float to absorb as much water as possible, about 30 seconds. Remove from water with a slotted spatula, allowing excess water to drain off. Transfer to prepared baking sheet, carefully brushing each cracker with melted butter. Be careful not to flatten cracker. Bake 15 minutes. Reduce oven temperature to 300 degrees and continue baking until golden brown, about 25 minutes. Cool on wire rack.

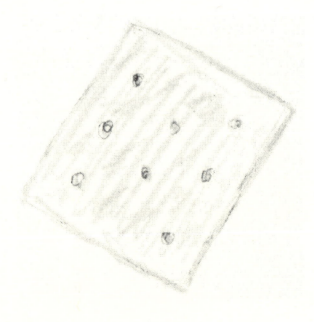

SPICED NUTS
Yield: 2 cups

This recipe is from Virginia Bloodgood (St. Martin's Church, Radnor). We all loved them – even John!

1 **egg white**
2 tablespoons cold **water**
½ cup granulated **sugar**
½ teaspoon **salt**
½ teaspoon **cinnamon**
¼ teaspoon powdered **cloves**
¼ teaspoon **allspice**
2 cups **pecans** or **walnuts**

Beat egg white slightly. Add water. Dissolve sugar in egg white mixture. Add salt, spices and blend. Dip nuts in this mixture, then place each nut flat side down on greased cookie sheet. Bake for 1 hour in a preheated 250 degree oven.

NOTE: I would check them from time to time if I were you!

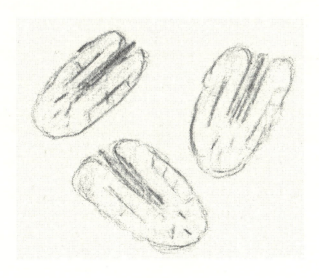

FATHER SMART'S CHICKEN LIVER PATÉ

Yield: 3–4 cups

We got this recipe first from Aunt Viv. It soon became known as Father Smart's Paté, as Dad made it every year for the Christmas Bazaar in Solebury. Always a sell-out!

3 tablespoons **butter**
½ cup finely chopped **onions**
2 tablespoons finely chopped **shallots**
1 small tart **apple**, peeled, cored, chopped coarsely
2-4 tablespoons **heavy cream**
3 tablespoons **butter**
1 pound **chicken livers**, cleaned, washed, cut in halves
10 ounces **butter**, softened to room temperature
2 teaspoons freshly squeezed **lemon juice**
2 teaspoons **salt**
¼ teaspoon freshly ground **black pepper**

Melt 3 tablespoons butter in large, heavy frying pan. Add onions and shallots and cook over moderate heat for 5-7 minutes, until onions are soft and lightly colored. Mix in apple and cook 3-4 minutes longer. Put 2 tablespoons cream in blender, add onion mixture when soft enough to mash with a spoon. Melt 3 more tablespoons butter, add livers, cook 3-4 minutes over brisk heat until brown on the outside, still slightly pink inside. Add livers and juices to blender. Blend at high speed, adding more cream if it clogs. COOL COMPLETELY. Very important!

Cream 10 ounces butter. Add cooled liver paste, a little at a time, beating thoroughly. Add lemon juice, salt and pepper. Taste and correct seasonings. Pack into any attractive quart-size glass or pottery dish or several smaller ones. Cover with plastic wrap and refrigerate 3-4 hours until firm or freeze for future use. Serve with French bread, pumpernickel, or Melba toast.

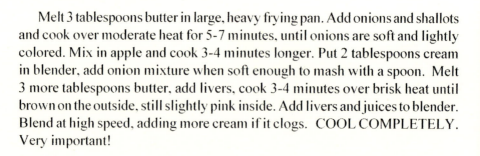

SOUP

I REMEMBER . . . when Mother served soup, it was usually the main course. Her vegetable soup with dumplings was wonderful – always made "from scratch." I don't think she ever used a can of broth or a bouillon cube!

But when I recall soup, there is one supper I shall never forget. It was in the dead of winter in North Dakota; days were short and it was very cold. On this particular day I had had a piano lesson several blocks away. When it was over, I trudged home, cold and tired and hungry. And it was already very dark.

Mother soon called us to the table – a simple meal of potatoes and dumplings, cooked, I believe, in whole milk (perhaps some cream, too, knowing Mother) and butter, I'm sure, the size of an egg. Well, I remember thinking, "this is the best meal in the whole world!" Couple that with the warm cozy home surrounded by family. "Best" is right!

Whenever I think of this particular day in my life, I am reminded of another story. When you children were 6 and 8 years old, we traveled for 35 days in Europe in our little Citroen. Because we felt quite poor, we ate cold food out of our picnic basket, 3 meals a day. One of those days we were traveling in Switzerland. It was cold and snowing and getting dark. Late in the afternoon Dad found us our accommodations for the night – and would you believe, it had a little kitchen.

Dad took you children and went searching for a market. You came home with many "tins" – which we opened and heated up. When we were through eating, John took a deep breath and said, "That was the best dinner I've ever had!" Hot is good.

BEAN SOUP

Yield: about 4 quarts

Warm and comforting on a cold winter's day!

1 pound small **navy beans**
1 **ham bone** or 2 **ham hocks**
1 large **onion**
2 cloves **garlic**
1 large can (28 ounces) **tomatoes**
juice of one **lemon**
salt and **pepper**

Wash 1 pound small navy beans thoroughly. Place in large pot, cover with water and soak overnight. (Today there is a "short-soak" method that is quite acceptable.) In the morning drain the beans and then add 2 quarts fresh water and the ham. You may have to add more as they cook – you don't want it too thick. So much of cooking is free-wheeling! Simmer slowly for about 2 hours. Add 1 large onion, chopped, 1 large can tomatoes, 2 cloves garlic, minced, juice of 1 lemon and salt and pepper to taste. Simmer for about an hour longer. Remove the meat from the bones and add it to the pot. I usually refrigerate the finished soup overnight. In the morning I can easily remove the congealed fat.

NOTE: An interesting variation is to use a variety of beans – as many as 7 different kinds are fun. In fact, you could call this Calico Soup and use:

cranberry beans	kidney	lentils	split peas
chick peas	red bean	pinto	black
great northern	limas	marrow	black-eyed peas

CARROT AND GINGER SOUP
Yield: 1 ½ quarts

This recipe is from John Root and has always been one of my favorites. Jeannie suggested that the soup should be a little on the "chunky" side and I agree. So don't over-blend!

6 tablespoons **butter**
1 large yellow **onion**
¼ cup finely chopped fresh **ginger**
3 cloves of **garlic**, minced
7 cups **chicken stock**
1 cup dry **white wine** or 1 additional cup of **chicken broth**
1 ½ pounds **carrots**, peeled and cut into ½ inch pieces
2 tablespoons fresh **lemon juice**
pinch of **curry powder** (optional)
salt and **pepper** to taste
garnish with chopped **chives** or **parsley**

Melt butter. Add onion, ginger and garlic. Saute 15 minutes. Add stock, wine and carrots. Heat to boiling and then simmer uncovered until the carrots are very tender, about 45 minutes. Puree in blender. Add lemon juice, curry powder, salt and pepper. Serve either hot or cold!

CHILLED FLORENTINE SOUP

Yield: 6 - 8 servings

Just as delicious hot! Keeps well in refrigerator for several days. Pretty color! This has been a favorite of mine for over 30 years.

3 tablespoons **butter**
½ cup chopped **onions**
2 – 10 ounce packages of frozen **chopped spinach**
3 cans (13 ¾ ounces each) **chicken broth**
salt and **pepper** to taste
dash of **nutmeg**
1 – 8 ounce package **Philadelphia cream cheese**

In a large skillet sauté onions in butter. Add spinach and cover. (No need to add any water). Cook over medium heat for 10 minutes or until leaves are wilted.. Add chicken broth, salt, pepper and nutmeg. Simmer 5 minutes. Cool slightly. Pour part of the soup at a time, together with a chunk of the cheese, into container of electric blender. Cover and whirl until smooth. Chill at least 4 hours.

ESCAROLE-GARLIC SOUP WITH CANNELINI BEANS

Yield: 4 generous servings

A delicious combination!

1 bunch **escarole** (about 1 pound)
¼ cup **olive oil**
5 to 6 medium cloves fresh **garlic**, finely minced
1 medium **onion**, sliced
2 quarts **chicken broth**
2 sprigs fresh **parsley**, chopped
1 can (16 ounces) white **cannelini beans**, drained and rinsed
freshly ground **black pepper** to taste
2 cups cooked **rice**
grated **Parmesan cheese**

Rinse and drain escarole to remove sand. Cut the leaves crosswise into long, thin pieces. Heat the olive oil in a large saucepan. Saute the escarole, garlic and onions for 5 minutes, stirring from time to time. Add ½ cup of the chicken broth, cover, reduce heat to low and simmer for 25 minutes. If liquid is absorbed too quickly, add more broth to avoid burning. Add the remaining broth, parsley, cannelini beans and pepper to taste. Cover and simmer 10 minutes longer. To serve, place ½ cup of the hot rice into each of 4 soup bowls; pour soup over. Pass Parmesan cheese at the table.

VEGETABLE SOUP
Yield: 4 quarts

When I was growing up, my mother usually made dumplings and cooked them in the soup just before serving. As we have become more calorie conscious through the years, I haven't always done that. However, these dumplings are an excellent addition to this soup. As you might have noticed, they are made the same way as cream puffs. John thought they were the best he'd ever eaten!

3 – 4 tablespoons good **vegetable oil**
chopped vegetables – you decide the amount.
Choose any or all of the following:

garlic	**rutabaga**	**onions**	**celery**
carrots	**turnip**	**cabbage**	**green beans**
corn	**potato** (or a handful of **macaroni** or **rice**)		

1 – 28 ounce can of **tomatoes**
 chicken or beef broth - enough to make a thin or a thicker soup
salt and **pepper**

Pour into your pot the vegetable oil – heat. Put in all your vegetables and cook them together for about 15 minutes. Add the broth and tomatoes and simmer for 2 or 3 hours. Add salt and pepper to taste.

Danish Dumplings
4 tablespoons **butter**
½ cup boiling **water**
2/3 cup **all-purpose flour**
1 teaspoon **salt**
2 **eggs**

Boil butter and water. Add flour and salt all at once, stirring continually until mixture leaves sides of pan. Cool slightly and then add the eggs, one at a time, beating well after each egg. The batter should be smooth and satiny. Drop by teaspoonful into boiling water or broth. Do not cover. They are usually done when they rise to the top. Eat one to check for doneness.

NOTE: My mother, of course, always made her own broth from scratch. Today we tend to use short-cuts. There are some good canned broths available!

FISH CHOWDER
Yield: 6 servings

This is one of Jeannie's recipes. Simply delicious! Couldn't be easier!

6 tablespoons **butter**
1 cup chopped **onion**
¾ cup chopped **parsley**
1 cup chopped **tomatoes**
1 1/3 cups cold **water**
2/3 cup **white wine**
2 pounds **cod**

Saute the butter and onion until translucent. Add the parsley and simmer for 2 minutes. Add the tomatoes and simmer for another 2 minutes. Add the water and wine and simmer for 10 minutes. Add the cod and simmer for 10 minutes or until it flakes easily with a fork.

SALADS AND SALAD DRESSINGS

I REMEMBER . . . when I was growing up, our "greens" meant Iceburg lettuce. And we had no fresh tomatoes in the winter months. Cole slaw and congealed salads were most popular. Fruit-flavored gelatins with real whipped cream were lovely to look at and actually very refreshing.

You children grew up with a much larger salad vocabulary. You knew the difference between endive and romaine, shitake and portobello mushrooms, alfalfa and bean sprouts. And your choice of salad dressings was endless. One of your all-time favorites was the Greek Salad.

GREEK SALAD

Yield: It's up to you!

Always a favorite!

The traditional Greek salad consists of greens (lettuce, chickory, escarole, romaine, endive, etc.) torn into bite-sized pieces, wedges of tomato, slices of cucumber, onion and green pepper, anchovies, Kalamata olives and feta cheese. Any or all of these ingredients may be used.

Rub a large salad bowl with garlic.
Add any or all of the above ingredients.
Add dressing (watch it – not too much) and toss gently.

The Dressing
1 part **lemon juice** or **wine vinegar**
3 parts **olive oil**
salt and **pepper**
optional: a sprinkling of **oregano** or **fresh mint** in season

Put all ingredients in a jar with a tight lid and shake vigorously.

OLD FASHIONED POTATO SALAD

Yield: 1 1/2 quarts

One day while talking with John about my cookbook, he said, "I hope you put in your potato salad!" So here it is, John!

It is hard to be precise in amounts. Tasting is good!

3-4 large **potatoes**, boiled in their skins
1 tablespoon **vinegar**
1 tablespoon **olive oil**
1 teaspoon **celery seed**
1/2 cup chopped **onion**
1/2 cup chopped **green pepper**
3 hard boiled **eggs**
mayonnaise

As soon as the potatoes are cool enough to handle, peel and cut into cubes in a large bowl. Sprinkle the vinegar, olive oil and celery seeds over the potatoes and let stand while you prepare the onions and peppers. Add the onions and peppers and chopped eggs to the potatoes. Add mayonnaise, enough to bind it together. It will need a little salt and pepper.

ROQUEFORT OR BLEU CHEESE DRESSING

Yield: approximately 1 pint

Now, I always free-wheel. Taste and decide whether you want a little more garlic, a touch more lemon juice, a bit more cheese!

1 cup **sour cream**
1 cup **mayonnaise**
1 ½ teaspoons **lemon juice**
1 clove **garlic**, minced
1 (1 ½ ounce) wedge **bleu cheese**, crumbled

Combine all ingredients and blend well.

Taste and enjoy!

KELSEY DRESSING
Yield: Approximately 1 quart

Daddy used to go to Minneapolis on business trips and he always rode the Great Northern! Mr. Kelsey, a friend of his, was a conductor on the railroad in the Midwest. This concoction was served in the dining car. Dad liked it and got the recipe – and forever after we called it Kelsey Dressing.

- 1 **egg yolk**
- 1 tablespoon **salad oil**
- 1 tablespoon **lemon juice**
- ½ tablespoon **dry mustard**
- ½ teaspoon **salt**
- ½ teaspoon **sugar**
- 1 pint **salad oil**
- 1 tablespoon hot **vinegar**
- 1 teaspoon prepared **mustard**
- 2 cloves **garlic**
- 1 can undiluted **tomato soup**, brought to a boil

Mix the first 6 ingredients and beat well. It will be very stiff. Add gradually the rest of the ingredients and beat thoroughly. If you like, you may strain to remove garlic. This will last for a long while in the refrigerator.

NOTE: The hot vinegar and boiling hot soup should make the egg "safe."

RICE SALAD PRIMAVERA

Yield: 12 to 14 servings

We usually served this with Chicken Tonnato – wonderful for a buffet supper!

- 1 cup uncooked **long-grain rice**
- 1 bunch **broccoli** (about 1 pound)
- ½ pound **snow peas**
- ½ pound **mushrooms**, thickly sliced
- 1 pint **cherry tomatoes**
- 1 sweet **red pepper**, cut into strips
- 1 sweet **green pepper**, cut into strips
- 4 **scallions** thickly sliced

Cook rice following package directions. Cool to room temperature. Wash and trim broccoli. Cut into bite-size pieces. Cook broccoli in saucepan of boiling salted water until crisp-tender. Drain. Snip off the tips and remove the strings from snow peas. Blanch. Combine rice, broccoli, snow peas, mushrooms, cherry tomatoes, red and green pepper strips and scallions in large salad bowl. Toss lightly.

Note: Blanch - To scald briefly in boiling water. Drain.

Dressing
1 cup **olive oil**
2 tablespoons **lemon juice**
2 tablespoons **tarragon vinegar**
2 cloves **garlic**, finely chopped
1 teaspoon **dry mustard**
salt and **pepper**

Combine oil, lemon juice, vinegar, garlic, mustard, salt and pepper in a screw top jar. Cover and shake well. Pour over rice mixture; toss until thoroughly coated. Refrigerate until serving time.

LUNCHEON DISHES

I REMEMBER... when Mother entertained her lady friends, it was mostly at afternoon parties. And I remember all the food – it was really a full meal in the middle of the afternoon! Today we serve the same kinds of food but two or three hours earlier – at "lunch time!"

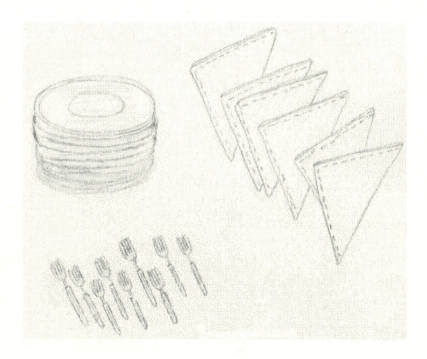

BRUSCHETTA

Yield: 4 servings or 8 first course

In Italy this is traditionally a workman's midday snack, but in my book it is food for the gods! Simply marvelous! Jeannie said she had this for lunch almost every day that she was in Rome – that was 6 months!

12 to 14 ripe **plum tomatoes**
2 tablespoons minced **garlic**
2 tablespoons minced **shallots**
1 cup fresh **basil leaves**
1 teaspoon fresh **lemon juice**
salt and ground **black pepper**, to taste
1/3 cup plus 1/4 cup **extra virgin olive oil**
3 cloves **garlic**, slivered
8 thick slices round peasant **bread**

Drop tomatoes in boiling water for a minute or two and then peel. Dice tomatoes and place in a bowl. Toss with the minced garlic and shallots. Coarsely chop the basil and add to the tomatoes with the lemon juice, salt and pepper, and 1/3 cup olive oil. Leave uncovered on counter top for two to three hours. Heat the ¼ cup olive oil in a small skillet and saute the slivered garlic until golden, 2 to 3 minutes. Remove the garlic and reserve the oil. Toast the bread. Arrange the slices on plates. Brush the oil over each slice, spoon the tomato mixture over the bread and serve immediately. Have some anchovies available for those who like them!

GREEK QUICHE
Yield: one 9 inch pie

This recipe is from Iris Leclair, a lovely lady and an excellent cook! She put on a cooking demonstration just for me!

1 **crust**, unbaked
2 bunches **scallions**, chopped
4 ounces **mushrooms**, chopped
1 package (10 ounces) **frozen spinach**, thawed
2 tablespoons fresh **parsley**, chopped
1 cup diced **ham**
seasoned salt and savory
olive oil
5 **eggs**
½ cup **milk or light cream**
¼ cup grated **Parmesan**
¼ pound **feta cheese**, crumbled
1 ½ cups shredded **mozzarella** or **Monterey Jack** cheese

Preheat oven to 375 degrees. Cover the bottom of a large fry pan with olive oil. Sauté gently onions and mushrooms. Squeeze as much moisture as you can from the spinach and add it to the pan. Add diced ham and seasonings. Sauté all together a few more minutes. Set aside. Beat together the eggs, cream, Parmesan and feta. Sprinkle ½ cup shredded mozzarella in the bottom of the pie shell. Pour enough egg mixture over shell to cover bottom. Cover with sautéed vegetables and ham. Sprinkle lightly with nutmeg and another ½ cup of shredded mozzarella. Pour rest of egg mixture over all. Sprinkle a few bread crumbs around edge of pie shell to prevent run-over. Bake 30-40 minutes. Ten minutes before it is done, sprinkle a little more cheese over all.

ITALIAN QUICHE
Yield: one 9 inch pie

Another winner from Iris Leclair. She invited me to her home to observe the making of this and the Greek Quiche. It was fun to visit with her.

1 **crust**, unbaked
5 **eggs**
½ cup **light cream**
½ cup **Parmesan cheese**, grated
1 medium sized **onion**, diced
4 ounces **mushrooms**, chopped
1 medium sized **zucchini**, diced
shredded **mozzarella**
pepperoni, thinly sliced
3 or 4 **Roma tomatoes**
chopped fresh **basil**
bread crumbs

Preheat oven to 350-375 degrees. Beat together the eggs, the light cream and the Parmesan cheese. Saute gently the onion, mushrooms and zucchini. Sprinkle some shredded cheese on crust. Pour 1/3 of egg mixture on crust. Sprinkle sautéed vegetables over egg mixture. Pour another 1/3 of egg mixture over vegetables. Sprinkle with more shredded cheese, layer pepperoni over all. Pour on rest of egg mixture and a little sprinkling of cheese on the entire surface. This should keep the tomatoes from falling through. Put a single layer of sliced tomato over all. (HINT: Let tomatoes stand on counter for a day or so before slicing to "dry out" a bit. Sprinkle chopped basil, Italian seasoning and Parmesan over all. Sprinkle lightly with bread crumbs. (This step too will absorb some of the moisture.) Bake 30-40 minutes. Add more shredded cheese and bake an additional 10 minutes.

MUSHROOM STRUDEL

Yield: 4 strudel bars

This is a "Radnor" recipe! A rather impressive presentation!

2 pounds sliced **mushrooms**
2 cloves **garlic**, pressed
½ cup (1 stick) **butter**
¼ cup **sherry**
salt and **pepper** to taste
4 tablespoons chopped **parsley**
4 tablespoons chopped **chives**
1 cup **sour cream**
½ pound **butter**, melted (or much less if you choose to use cooking spray).
1 ½ cups dry **bread crumbs**
8 **phyllo** leaves

Chop enough parsley and chives to measure 4 tablespoons each; reserve. Sauté 2 pounds sliced mushrooms and 2 large cloves garlic in 1 stick butter in a large skillet 3 minutes. Add ¼ cup sherry. Continue cooking, stirring constantly, until liquid has evaporated. Add salt, pepper, chopped parsley and chopped chives. Remove from heat; add 1 cup dairy sour cream; cover skillet; Reserve. Melt ½ pound butter (or less if you are going to use some cooking spray). Preheat oven to 350 degrees. Lay a dampened towel on the table and remove 2 phyllo leaves from package. Working quickly, put one leaf on towel. Paint it with butter, going right to the edges, or spray. Sprinkle with 3 tablespoons dry bread crumbs. Top with second leaf. Paint with butter again, or spray, and sprinkle with 3 tablespoons dry bread crumbs. Leaving 2 inch margins on sides, pile one quarter of the mushroom mixture along bottom edge. Fold in margins. Holding the lower corners of the towel tautly, flip the strudel over and over until you are at the end. Lift the strudel onto your waiting buttered rimmed baking pan. Paint with butter and cover loosely with waxed paper while making remaining bars. Remove paper and bake in oven for 20 minutes or until golden brown. Serve warm. NOTE: This is a wonderful "make ahead." The completed un-baked bars can be frozen successfully. They need not be thawed before baking.

VEGETABLES

I REMEMBER . . . in our home in Williston we had fresh vegetables in season – and lots of them. During the winter months we were served vegetables from the can. Frozen vegetables came later. Mother used to tell us that when she was a child, they waited and waited for corn season. And when it was "just right," they cooked the ears in the wash boiler. Corn, dripping with butter, was their entire meal!

Since cholesterol and calories have become such important words in our vocabulary, we have gotten used to eating our vegetables unadorned. But in days gone by, we enjoyed the richness of sauces and cheese and butter in and with and under our vegies.

Our regimen today is more healthful to be sure, but I think it must be all right to indulge every now and again. Twice baked potatoes, anyone?

Note: I'm not sure either of you has ever seen what Mother called a "wash boiler." It was a large oval-shaped galvanized metal container with a wooden handle at each end. Housewives used these to boil water for washing clothes. I remember my Aunt Hilda on the farm put her "boiler" on a small stove in the wash house Sunday night so it would be good and hot for early Monday morning laundry. My Mother always had hot and cold running water so she was spared this chore.

DELICIOUS ZUCCHINI CASSEROLE
Yield: 10 servings

We certainly ate a lot of zucchini when you were growing up. When we had it in our own garden, they seemed to multiply and mature overnight! This recipe is easy to make for large crowds. A good picnic dish.

Preheat oven to 350 degrees. Place in a large buttered casserole in layers: sliced **zucchini**, sliced **onions**, sliced **tomatoes** Sprinkle each layer with seasoned **bread crumbs** and dab with **butter.** Repeat layers. Bake until tender and brown.

RED CABBAGE
Yield: 10 - 12 servings

From Doug Heisler, a young man who worshiped at Holy Trinity for a time. He was a hotel manager who liked his kitchen best of all!

1 head of **red cabbage** (2-3 pounds)
4 slices of **bacon**, chopped
6 tablespoons finely chopped **onion**
2 **Granny Smith apples**, peeled, cored and thinly sliced
½ cup **golden raisins**
¼ teaspoon **salt**
½ teaspoon freshly ground **pepper**
½ cup dry **red wine**
¼ cup **red wine vinegar**
2 tablespoons **dark brown sugar**
¼ cup **red currant jelly**
¼ teaspoon each **nutmeg** and **cinnamon**

Shred the cabbage and soak in cold water. Cook the bacon in a skillet until some of the fat is rendered. Add onions and saute until wilted. Lift the red cabbage from the water, leaving it moist. Place in an enameled iron pot; cover and simmer for 10 minutes. Add bacon and onions and the remaining ingredients and mix with the cabbage. Cover and simmer very slowly for 1 ¼ hours.

GNOCCHI IN BASIL BUTTER
Yield: 8 – 10 servings

This is a wonderful substitute for potatoes, rice or pasta. John Root, our neighbor and friend in Solebury, thought these gnocchi were the best he'd ever eaten --and coming from John Root, who had been around, we considered this quite a compliment!

Gnocchi
4 cups **milk**
2 teaspoons **salt**
1 cup **farina**
¼ cup sweet butter
6 tablespoons grated **Parmesan**
freshly ground **pepper**

Put milk in a heavy saucepan and bring to a boil. Add salt and farina and cook until very thick. Remove from stove and add ¼ cup butter and 3 tablespoons Parmesan cheese. Rinse jelly roll pan in cold water. Spread mixture evenly. Let cool. Refrigerate 1 hour.

Basil Butter
6 tablespoons **butter**, softened
2 tablespoons fresh **basil**, chopped
2 cloves **garlic**, minced
1 tablespoon **parsley**, chopped

Combine thoroughly. With cookie cutter cut out rounds and place domino fashion in a large buttered baking dish or cookie sheet with rim. Place bits of basil butter all over and sprinkle with the remaining Parmesan cheese. Place in a preheated 350 degree oven for 30 minutes.

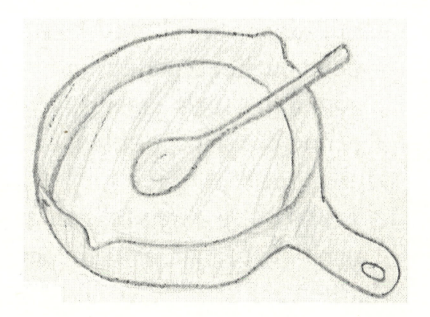

ROASTED AUTUMN VEGETABLES

Yield: It's up to you.

A nice variation on the vegetable theme. Attractive and delicious!

¼ cup **butter**
1 tablespoon fresh or 1 teaspoon **dried sage leaves**
1 clove **garlic**, crushed
½ pound **Brussels sprouts**, cut in halves
½ pound **parsnips**, peeled, cut into 2 inch pieces (remove the core if it is tough)
¼ pound **baby carrots**, peeled
1 small **butternut squash**, peeled and seeded, cut into 1 inch pieces

Preheat oven to 375 degrees. Melt butter in small saucepan; stir in sage and garlic. Place vegetables in rectangular pan 13x9x2 inches. Pour butter mixture over vegetables; stir to coat. Bake 25 to 30 minutes, stirring occasionally., until vegetables are crisp-tender.

NOTE: Jeannie recommends roasting almost any vegetable – even asparagus. She simply sprays the vegetables with olive or canola oil, eliminating the butter. Delicious.

TWICE BAKED POTATOES
Yield: You choose!

You children LOVED these potatoes. I guess we all did!

baking potatoes
butter
sour cream
salt and **white pepper**
paprika

Scrub as many baking potatoes as you care to make. Try to get them as even in size and shape as you can. Bake them in a hot oven. When they are tender, remove them from the oven. Slice off the top of each, about an inch. Scoop out the potatoes being careful not to break the shell. With an electric beater beat until the potatoes are very smooth. When all the lumps are gone, add butter and sour cream, equally, until you have the consistency that you like. It is important to get all the lumps out before you add the cream and butter – you can't get rid of them after the additions! Fill the shells, pile them high. It is nice to use a cake decorator for the final touch. Fill a tube with mashed potatoes and decorate. Sprinkle with paprika. Bake again for about 30 minutes or until lightly brown.

NOTE: These freeze beautifully! Fill the shells, decorate, and freeze. Thaw before baking.

CASSEROLES AND MAIN DISHES

I REMEMBER . . . Mother's casserole recipes were few – macaroni and cheese, chop suey, spaghetti or elbow macaroni with homemade hamburger/tomato sauce. This dish was usually mixed all together and baked until a wonderful crust formed on top. She also made a ground ham and noodle dish that I adored.

Today, with more informal buffet suppers than sit-down dinners, casseroles are "in." During our time at Holy Trinity, we often entertained Club Trinity (30-35 young adults) for supper. For those occasions we tried a lot of new recipes – some we tossed and some we kept! It was fun.

BEEF STUFFED CABBAGE ROLLS

Yield: 8 servings

Peasant fare, but fit for a king! This was often my contribution to a church pot luck supper. A delicious and inexpensive cold-weather treat!

1 pound **ground beef**
1/2 cup uncooked **rice**
1 **onion**, minced
1 **egg**
salt and **pepper** to taste
1 **cabbage** (about 4 pounds)
1 pound **sauerkraut**, undrained
1 large can whole **tomatoes** (28 ounces)
1/4 cup **butter**
1 1/2 cups boiling **water**

Mix first 5 ingredients. Add as much salt and pepper as you like. Cut core out of cabbage to a depth of 3 inches. Put cabbage into a large kettle of boiling water on high heat. With tongs, remove about 20 leaves as they wilt and let them stand until cool enough to handle. Carefully cut out coarsest part of rib of cabbage. Cool remaining cabbage and cut coarsely or chop. Preheat oven to 350 degrees. Put half of chopped cabbage into a large buttered casserole. Put a spoonful of meat mixture in center of each leaf; roll up, tucking ends under and then put them on top of cabbage in casserole. Top with remaining cabbage, sauerkraut, tomatoes and butter. Add the boiling water. Cover and bake for about an hour and a half. (Add more tomatoes and liquid if it appears dry).

NOTE: This tastes even better the second day!

CHICKEN CASSEROLE
Yield: 8 to 10 servings

This recipe came from Mrs. Drorbaugh's kitchen assistant. It is really very, very good – the combination of flavors is out of this world!

1 – 6 pound **roasting chicken**
2 pounds fresh **mushrooms**
2 pounds **pork sausage links**
½ pint **heavy cream**

Stuff chicken with a large onion and some celery and roast in an oven cooking bag. Save the juices. Fry sausages and set aside. Sauté sliced mushrooms in butter. Preheat oven to 350 degrees. Slice chicken and layer in a good-sized casserole the chicken, sausages and mushrooms. Pour juices from all preparations over the baking dish and then add the cream. Bake about 30 minutes. Serve with rice.

Note: Do not bake too long ahead of serving!

CHICKEN/TURKEY TONNATO
Yield: 8 – 10 servings

Veal Tonnato is a famous Italian summer dish, but I almost like Chicken/Turkey Tonnato better – certainly the price! Jeannie made this for Club Trinity (36 young adults) in May 1988. It was a smashing success with the Rice Primavera (the recipe may be found in the salad section of this book).

3 pounds **turkey breast OR** same amount of **boneless chicken breasts**
1 **onion** stuck with a **clove**
1 **carrot**
1 stick **celery**
2 –3 fillets of **anchovy**
½ sour **pickle**
1 can **tuna fish** (6 ounces)
2 cloves **garlic**
thyme, parsley, salt, pepper
1 pint **white wine**
½ cup **olive oil**
a little **water**, if necessary

Put all the ingredients in a heavy pot; cover and simmer until tender. Cool in juices. Remove turkey or chicken and slice. (At this point place in a covered container, moisten with a little juice and refrigerate.) Remove vegetables and tuna fish from the broth and blend, adding some juice to make it a consistency of a thin sauce. Mix this sauce with an equal amount of mayonnaise. Sharpen with lemon juice. When ready to serve, spoon sauce over the chicken/turkey and garnish the platter in any way you choose.

GINNY'S SAUSAGE CASSEROLE
Yield: 8 servings

Ginny Saunders served this on one of my "overnights" in Solebury. It came from her mother, Mrs. Swain. It is delicious and easy and can be prepared ahead. What more can one ask?

1 pound **pork sausage**
1 cup **rice**
2 packages (2 ounces each) dehydrated **chicken noodle soup**
¼ cup chopped **onion**
1 cup sliced **celery**
2 ½ cups **water**
1 tablespoon **soy sauce**
½ cup toasted slivered blanched **almonds**

Brown sausage in an ungreased skillet. Pour off fat as it accumulates. Remove from heat when done. Mix together sausage, rice, soup, onion, celery and place in a 2 quart casserole. If you are making this ahead - refrigerate. (It may even be made the day before serving.) When ready to bake, mix soy sauce with water. Add this and the almonds to the casserole and mix gently. Cover and bake 1 hour in a 350 degree oven.

NOTE: To toast almonds, spread on baking sheet and put in a 325 degree oven for perhaps 10 minutes, shaking the pan every few minutes. Watch carefully because they burn easily.

DO AHEAD RISOTTA

Yield: 10 to 15 servings

After Jeannie discovered this recipe, we used it many times at buffet parties. We especially liked the fact that it can be made ahead of time. It is essential that you use Italian short-grain rice; arborio is a widely available variety.

6 tablespoons (3/4 stick) **butter**, plus more for pan
½ cup **bread crumbs**
10 cups **chicken stock**
1 **onion** finely chopped
2 cloves **garlic**, finely chopped
1 cup finely chopped fresh **Italian parsley**
3 cups **arborio rice**
1 cup dry **white wine**
½ cup grated **Parmesan**, (plus more for garnish)
salt and freshly ground **pepper**

Butter an 8 inch springform pan and coat with bread crumbs, shaking off excess. Set aside. In a large saucepan, heat stock to boiling, then lower to a simmer. In a large, heavy saucepan over low heat, melt 3 tablespoons of the butter. Add onion, garlic, and about 2/3 cup of the parsley and cook until soft and transparent. Increase heat to medium and add rice. Stir well to coat all the grains. Add wine and simmer, stirring constantly, until mostly absorbed, about 3 minutes. Add remaining stock a half cup at a time, stirring constantly. Always wait until stock is nearly absorbed before adding the next. Continue until rice is creamy but firm, about 15 to 20 minutes. You must taste rice to judge doneness. Remaining parsley may be added about halfway through cooking time. Stir in remaining 3 tablespoons butter, Parmesan, and salt and pepper to taste. Pour into prepared pan, cool completely, and refrigerate overnight. Heat oven to 400 degrees. Bake for about 30 minutes, or until heated through (test by inserting a knife into the center for 15 seconds and checking its temperature). Unmold onto a large platter, sprinkle grated Parmesan over the top, slice into wedges and serve.

GRATIN OF COD, POTATOES AND TOMATOES

Yield: 6 servings

This is a "Jeannie Recipe" – and simply delicious.

1 ½ pounds fresh **cod** fillets, cut 1 inch thick
2 large ripe **tomatoes** (about 1 pound), peeled and sliced
3 small baking **potatoes** (about 1 pound), peeled and sliced
½ teaspoon **salt**
Freshly ground black **pepper**, to taste

Preheat oven to 350 degrees F. Lightly oil bottom and sides of a shallow 2 quart baking dish. Cut fish to fit in two layers. Spread 1/3 of the tomatoes in prepared dish, top with 1/2 of the fish, then 1/2 potatoes, sprinkling each layer with salt and pepper. Top with ½ the remaining tomatoes, the remaining fish, and remaining potatoes. Cover with rest of tomatoes.

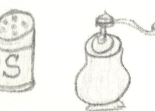

1/3 cup dry **white wine**
3 tablespoons **olive oil**
1 tablespoon **water**
Mix these ingredients and pour over top.

Crumb Topping
1/2 cup dry **bread crumbs**, preferably freshly made
1/3 cup minced **Italian parsley**
2 cloves **garlic**, minced
1/4 teaspoon **salt**
1/8 teaspoon freshly ground **pepper**

Combine and scatter evenly over the top. Cover dish with foil and bake for 1 hour; uncover and bake another 10 minutes or until potatoes and fish are tender.

LUCIE FARAMELLI'S LASAGNE
Yield: enough for a 9 x 13 inch pan

Dad and I enjoyed this with Lucy and her family more times than we can count.

Brown equal amounts of hamburger and mild Italian sausaage. Add equal amounts of tomato sauce and tomato paste, plus minced garlic, salt, pepper and oregano to taste. Simmer all of the above for 1 to 1 ½ hours. Cook lasagne noodles. Drain. Fill a 9 x 13 inch rectangular pan with alternate layers of noodles, sliced Mozarella cheese, ricotta cheese, meat sauce and grated Parmesan, ending with a layer of Parmesan. Make 3 layers because Lucy says it tastes best that way! Bake at 375 degrees for 20 minutes or until brown and bubbly.

NOTE: If you are going to freeze it, bake it first.

OLD FASHIONED MEAT LOAF
Yield: 14 – 16 servings

This was served at a big Club Trinity Do. Everyone wanted "seconds!"

2 pounds **beef**, ground twice
1 pound **pork shoulder**, ground twice
1 pound **veal shoulder**, ground twice
1 large **onion**, grated
2 **carrots**, finely shredded
4 to 6 cloves **garlic**, finely chopped
2 teaspoons **salt**
2 teaspoons **Dijon mustard**
1 teaspoon freshly ground **black pepper**
1 teaspoon crushed **rosemary**
¼ teaspoon **nutmeg**
½ teaspoon **Tabasco**
3 **eggs**, slightly beaten
¾ cup fresh **bread crumbs** soaked in ½ **cup milk**
12 strips **bacon** or **salt pork**

Preheat oven to 350 degrees. Combine the meats, grated onion and carrots, and seasonings and blend well. Mix in the eggs and soaked crumbs, combining thoroughly. Make a bed of bacon or salt pork strips in a shallow baking pan, reserving 4 or 5 for the top of the loaf. Form the meat mixture into a firm loaf with your hands and place it on the bed of bacon or salt pork. Put remaining strips across the top. Bake for 1 ½ to 2 hours, depending on how thick you have made the loaf, and baste several times with the pan juices. If you want to serve the meat loaf cold, wrap it tightly in foil and weight it as it cools, until firm. It will taste rather like a French country pate'.

THIS IS A NICE LIGHT TOMATO SAUCE TO BE SERVED WITH THE MEATLOAF WHEN PRESENTED HOT

28 ounce can whole **tomatoes** in puree
2 small **onions**, sliced
salt and freshly ground **black pepper** to taste
1 teaspoon dried **basil**
4 tablespoons **butter**

Cook the tomatoes, onions, salt, pepper and basil over medium-high heat for 20 minutes, stirring frequently, breaking up the tomatoes with a wooden spoon. Add the butter and continue to cook it until it melts. (Now I have often eliminated the butter and it tastes just fine!)

NOTE: The most delicious meat loaves are made with a combination of ground beef, veal and pork. The veal adds a gelatinous quality and the pork richness and fat, which keeps the meat loaf juicy. Incidentally, it should not be baked in a loaf pan. A meat loaf if molded and baked free form on a bed of bacon or salt pork sheds excess fat and makes a more firmly textured loaf, whereas, if baked in a loaf pan, it becomes much too moist and is sometimes not easily sliced.

RICOTTA CREPES UNDER MEAT-MUSHROOM SAUCE

Yield: 12 crepes

I must tell you that this recipe made quite a hit in Solebury when I made them for a Vestry Party – in the early '70's. I gave some to John Root and he thought they were so good and unusual that he bought me a crepe maker!

ALL-PURPOSE CREPES
1 cup **milk**
1/3 cup **water**
3 **eggs**
3 tablespoons **butter**, melted
1 cup all-purpose **flour**
1 tablespoon **sugar**
¼ teaspoon **salt**

Put the milk, water, eggs and melted butter in the blender – or use a rotary beater. Add the flour, sugar and salt and either blend or beat until smooth. Strain and let stand for an hour. Heat a heavy 7 inch nonstick skillet until quite hot. Pour in 3 tablespoons batter, then quickly tilt the pan so the batter spreads evenly, forming a crepe. Cook until lightly brown, 30 to 45 seconds; then turn and cook another 15 seconds. Repeat, using the remaining batter. As you finish, stack them between sheets of waxed paper. You can make these up to 2 days ahead.

FILLING
1 pound **ricotta cheese**
¼ pound **Monterey Jack OR Muenster cheese**, shredded
¼ teaspoon ground **nutmeg**
1/8 teaspoon **salt**
coarsely ground black **pepper**
2 tablespoons **butter**, melted
2 tablespoons grated **Parmesan cheese**

Stir together first five ingredients and spread one-twelfth of mixture in about a 4 inch circle in center of each crepe and roll. Arrange filled and rolled crepes in single layer in shallow buttered baking tray with rim. Brush with melted butter and sprinkle with the Parmesan cheese. (At this point they may be frozen and thawed before baking). Preheat the oven to 350 degrees and bake for about 12 minutes or until bubbly. Lift two crepes onto each warm serving plate and top with the sauce. Offer black pepper to grind on top.

MEAT-MUSHROOM SAUCE

½ pound bulk **pork sausage**
1 pound **ground beef**
1 large **onion**, chopped
3 large cloves **garlic**, minced
½ cup chopped **parsley**
½ pound fresh **mushrooms**, sliced
1 - 6 ounce can **tomato paste**
1 - 28 ounce can whole **tomatoes** in thick puree (preferably Roma)
12 ounces of **water** (fill the tomato paste can twice)
1 teaspoon **salt**
1 teaspoon ground **sage**
1 teaspoon crumbled dried **rosemary**
½ teaspoon each dried **marjoram, thyme** and coarsely ground **black pepper**

In a large thick kettle slowly brown sausage; add ground beef and brown. Add onions and sauté until limp. Add garlic, parsley and mushrooms and stir to coat with meat drippings. Stir in remaining ingredients. Cover loosely and simmer, stirring occasionally, 2 hours, or until reduced to a thick sauce consistency. Add a little more water if it seems too thick. Skim off any excess fat.

NOTE: It is good to make this ahead so that you can refrigerate it. It will be easy then to remove the congealed fat. Or you may cook it thoroughly and freeze it. Before using, thaw and slowly reheat.

RICE-STUFFED CORNISH HENS

Yield: 1 hen per guest

I served these with beautiful large asparagus spears and baby glazed carrots on our Lenox dinner plates. Pretty!

- ¾ cup chopped **onion**
- ¾ cup chopped **celery**
- ½ cup **butter**
- 3 cups cooked **rice**
- ¾ cup **raisins**
- 1/3 cup chopped **walnuts**
- 2 tablespoons **lemon juice**
- ¾ teaspoon ground **cinnamon**
- 1 teaspoon **salt**
- 1/8 teaspoon **pepper**
- 6 **Cornish game hens** (about 20 ounces each)

In a skillet, saute onion and celery in 3 tablespoons butter until tender; remove from the heat. Add rice, raisins, walnuts, lemon juice, cinnamon, salt and pepper; mix well. Preheat oven to 375 degrees. Stuff hens and carefully truss the wings and legs. Soften the remaining butter and rub over skins. Place on a rack in a large shallow baking pan. Bake uncovered for 2 hours or until the juices run clear. Turn, breast down, for part of the time so the whole bird becomes wonderfully brown. AND BASTE COMPLETELY EVERY 10 MINUTES! Remove hens to platter and keep warm. Pour off any fat from the roasting pan. Scrape all the good brown bits loose, add a little water and boil gently for a few minutes. Season. Serve this good sauce in a separate bowl.

SAUSAGE-WILD RICE CASSEROLE
Yield: 6 to 8 servings

This is one of the easiest and best recipes for a crowd that I know.

1 pound **bulk sausage**
½ pound **mushrooms**, sliced
1 cup chopped **onions**
1 cup sliced **celery**
1 can (8 ounces) sliced **water chestnuts**
1 ½ cups **water**
1 package **Uncle Ben's Wild Rice Mix** (original recipe) 6 ounces
½ teaspoon **thyme**
½ teaspoon **marjoram**

Preheat oven to 350 degrees. Brown the sausage in an ungreased skillet. Drain off all but 2 tablespoons of the accumulated fat. Add the mushrooms, onions and celery and brown lightly. Combine all ingredients in a 2 quart casserole with a lid. Bake, covered, for 1 ½ hours.

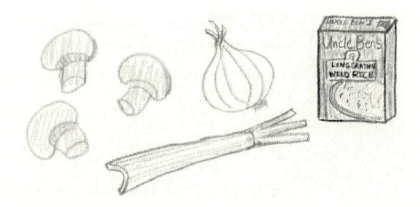

ALL READY SPAGHETTI

Yield: 4 generous servings

Really a nifty last-minute recipe. You'll never miss the meat!

2 cups **parsley**, stripped from the stems **OR**
1 cup **parsley** and 1 cup fresh **basil**
1/2 teaspoon **pepper**
2 cloves **garlic**, minced
1/2 cup **olive oil**
1/2 pound thin **spaghetti**
2 tablespoons **butter**
1/4 cup chopped **pecans** or **walnuts**
1/2 cup grated **Parmesan cheese**

Blend the first five ingredients at high speed. Occasionally you'll have to push it down the sides with a rubber scraper. Cook and drain spaghetti. Mix it well with 2 tablespoons butter. Add ¼ cup of chopped pecans or walnuts and ½ cup of grated Parmesan cheese. Add the parsley sauce and serve. Be sure it is hot through and through.

TERIAKI MARINADE FOR LONDON BROIL
Yield: 8 to 10 servings

This recipe is from Alice Doering from St. Martin's, Radnor. A favorite of Jeannie's.

4 pound **London Broil**
¾ cup **oil**
¼ cup **honey**
¼ cup **soy sauce**
2 tablespoons **vinegar**
1 large clove **garlic**
1 ½ teaspoons **ginger**
3-4 **scallions**, chopped
dash of **pepper**

Blend all ingredients, except beef, in blender. Marinate beef for 24 to 36 hours. From time to time poke meat with fork and turn. Grill until medium rare. Turn once. Hold the knife at a slight angle and slice - with the grain - very thin. (Slicing in this way will help retain the juices.)

VEAL STEW
Yield: 6 - 8 servings

Now this is an original! I served it several times to guests and they always wanted the recipe!

2 ½ pounds **veal cubes** (1 ½ - 2 inch pieces)
½ - ¾ cup **flour**
2 tablespoons **olive oil** (add a little more if needed)
1 medium **onion** chopped
4 large garlic **cloves**, minced
1 – 28 ounce can **tomatoes** in thick puree
1 ½ to 2 cups **beef broth**
2 tablespoons fresh **marjoram** or 2 teaspoons dried
2 teaspoons fresh **thyme** or 1 teaspoon dried
1 **bay leaf**
salt and **pepper** to taste
1 pound small **boiling onions**, cooked
2 – 14 or 16 ounce cans **artichoke hearts**, quartered
2 teaspoons **lemon juice**
1 – 14 ounce can pitted **Kalamata olives**
fresh chopped **parsley**

Heat oil in large heavy pan. Flour veal cubes and brown in batches on all sides and transfer veal to plate. Using another frying pan, quickly saute 1 medium onion, chopped, and 4 large garlic cloves, minced, in a small amount of oil or butter. In a casserole put the veal and any juice from the plate. Add the onions and garlic, the tomatoes, beef broth and spices. Cook gently until the veal is tender, 2 to 2 1/2 hours. When cool, refrigerate for several hours or overnight. Remove any accumulated fat. Remove veal and cook down the liquid until it has been reduced to 2 to 2 ½ cups. Return meat to the sauce and add the artichoke hearts, lemon juice and olives. Simmer until it is hot through. Sprinkle with the parsley before serving.

QUICK BREADS

I REMEMBER . . . these always seemed to be the perfect offering to friends and neighbors. They were easy to make and good to eat!

Most of our breads were delicious as they were, but we often slathered the slices with butter or cream cheese.

COFFEE KUCHEN
Yield: 2 dozen muffins

This recipe came from a secretary at St. Paul's Church in Westfield, NJ, a long time ago. You do remember, don't you, that it was in this church that Marie met Jack and they lived happily ever after.

3 cups all-purpose **flour**, sifted
3 teaspoons **baking powder**
1 teaspoon **salt**
2 cups **brown sugar**, firmly packed
1 cup **butter** (or ½ cup butter and ½ cup margarine)
½ cup very strong cold **coffee**
½ cup **evaporated milk**
¼ teaspoon **baking soda**
2 beaten **eggs**
1 teaspoon **cinnamon**

Preheat oven to 350 degrees and grease muffin pans. Sift together flour, baking powder, salt and brown sugar. Cut in butter (or butter and margarine). Reserve 1 cup for topping. Combine coffee, milk and soda and add to remaining flour mixture. Mix thoroughly. Add beaten eggs. Spoon into muffin tins, filling half full. Put reserved mixture on top of batter and sprinkle with cinnamon. Bake for about 25 minutes. Test for doneness. Remove from pans immediately and cool on racks.

CRANBERRY WALNUT BREAD
Yield: 3 – 9x5 loaves

This is the BEST cranberry bread I have ever eaten. The recipe came from Doug Heisler, a young man who used to come every now and then to Holy Trinity.

3 cups all-purpose **flour**
2 cups granulated **sugar**
2 teaspoons **baking powder**
2 teaspoons **baking soda**
1 teaspoon **salt**
2 teaspoons **cinnamon**
2 teaspoons **vanilla**
1 (12 ounce) bag fresh **cranberries**
1 cup chopped **walnuts**
1 cup **vegetable oil**
4 **eggs** beaten

Combine all ingredients in the order given. Bake in greased and floured 9x5 inch bread pans in a preheated 325 degree oven for about 40 minutes. Test for doneness. Remove from pans and cool on racks.

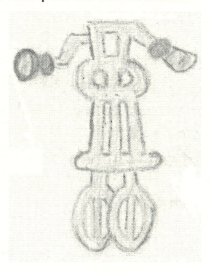

DATE AND NUT BREAD
Yield: 1 – 9x5 loaf

This is Charles Robinson's sister's recipe. It is delicious – dark and moist. A little cream cheese sandwiched between two small slices makes a lovely addition to any tea table.

- 1 teaspoon **baking soda**
- 1 cup boiling **water**
- 1 cup chopped **dates**
- ½ cup chopped **walnuts**
- 1 teaspoon **butter**
- 1 **egg**, beaten
- ½ teaspoon **vanilla**
- 1 cup all purpose **flour**, sifted
- 1 cup granulated **sugar**
- ½ teaspoon **salt**

Add soda to boiling water and pour over dates and nuts. Add butter and cool. Add beaten egg and vanilla. Mix flour, salt and sugar. Add date and nut mixture to dry ingredients. Bake in greased loaf tin lined on the bottom with waxed paper. The waxed paper is important! Bake 1 hour at 350 degrees.

DELICIOUS BAKING POWDER BISCUITS

Yield: 8-10 biscuits

Many, many years ago I entered this in a Pillsbury Baking Contest. Though I didn't win, trust me, they are very, very good!

2 cups all-purpose **flour**
5 teaspoons **baking powder**
1 teaspoon **salt**
1 cup **sour cream**

Mix batter thoroughly but gently. Pat out on floured surface to the thickness you desire. Cut out rounds with a biscuit cutter or use a sharp knife to cut squares. Bake for 10 to 12 minutes in a preheated 425 degree oven. Check – perhaps they are not quite brown enough – so bake a minute or two more!

GOUGÉRE

Yield: 6 to 8 servings

Do you recognize this? It is actually just a variation on the basic cream puff recipe. It is pretty as a picture and quite delicious. Fill the center, if you wish, with creamed chicken or turkey or whatever – and you have a lovely luncheon dish.

6 tablespoons **butter**
1 cup **water**
1 teaspoon **salt**
1 cup sifted all-purpose **flour**
4 **eggs**
8 ounces **Swiss cheese**

Bring to a boil: 6 tablespoons butter, 1 cup water and 1 teaspoon salt. Put in 1 cup sifted flour all at once. Stir until the mixture leaves the sides of the pot and becomes one large lump. Remove from fire and transfer to a mixing bowl. Cool slightly. Beat in 4 eggs, one at a time. Beat thoroughly after the addition of each egg. Stir into the mixture 8 ounces (minus 3 tablespoons) of Swiss Cheese in julienne or dice. Make a ring about 5 inches across on a lightly sprayed cookie sheet. Sprinkle remaining cheese on top and refrigerate over night. Bake at 425 degrees about 45 minutes. Check after about 30 minutes – you may want to turn it down a bit. Place on rack to cool slightly. Serve warm.

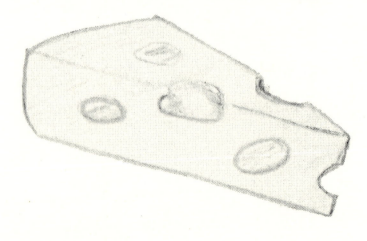

JEANNIE'S GRAHAM MUFFINS
Yield: 18 muffins

Lilly Magnuson, house-mother for Lutheran students at Bemidji State College, gave this recipe to me years and years ago. And there is no doubt about it, this recipe has been used more times than any other in this collection. It has served us well!

3 cups **whole wheat flour**
1 cup **brown sugar**
1 teaspoon **salt**
2 teaspoons **soda**
1 cup **raisins, dates** or **nuts**
2 cups sour **milk**

Mix all the dry ingredients together. Add the sour milk and mix well. Spoon into the greased muffin tins. Bake 20 minutes in a preheated 350 degree oven. Remove from pan immediately and cool on racks.

NOTE 1: To make sour milk, simply put 2 tablespoons vinegar in your 2 cup measuring glass and fill with milk. In a minute or so you will have very sour milk.

NOTE 2: Jeannie often made these muffins using 2 cups whole wheat flour and 1 cup oatmeal.

LEMON BREAD
Yield: 1 – 9x5 loaf pan

This is a delicious lemon bread and I think the secret is the 1 tablespoon of lemon extract in addition to the fresh lemon juice. From the files of Iris Leclair, a Wickenburg friend.

1 ½ cups granulated **sugar**
6 tablespoons **butter**
2 extra large **eggs**
1 tablespoon **lemon extract**
½ cup **milk**
1 ½ cups unsifted **flour**
½ teaspoon **salt**
1 ½ teaspoons **baking powder**
Grated rind of one **lemon**
3 tablespoons fresh **lemon juice**

Preheat oven to 350 degrees. Cream together 1 cup granulated sugar and the butter. Add slightly beaten eggs, lemon extract and milk. Mix well. Sift flour, salt and baking powder and add this and lemon rind to the creamed mixture. Mix until smooth. Grease and flour one 9x5 loaf pan. Fill with prepared batter. Bake about 40 minutes until golden brown and a toothpick inserted comes out clean. Mix remaining ½ cup of sugar with 3 tablespoons of lemon juice and pour over top of bread while still in the pan. Be sure that it soaks in. Return to oven and bake 5 – 8 minutes more or until glaze is absorbed. Cool on rack for about 10 minutes. Run spatula around edge to loosen and remove bread from pan. Cool completely should you wish to freeze it.

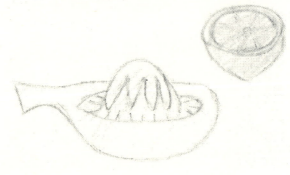

MY BEST GINGERBREAD

Yield: 9 large squares

Well named! It is unequivocally the best! It has survived a lot of years – Mother used to make this when I was a little girl!

½ cup granulated **sugar**
½ cup **butter** or **margarine**
1 **egg**, beaten
1 cup **molasses**
2 ½ cups sifted all-purpose **flour**
1 ½ teaspoon **baking soda**
1 teaspoon **cinnamon**
1 teaspoon **ginger**
½ teaspoon **cloves**
½ teaspoon **salt**
1 cup hot **water**

Preheat oven to 350 degrees and grease and flour a 9x9x2 inch pan. Cream thoroughly the butter and sugar. Add the beaten egg and molasses. Beat in all of the dry ingredients. Add the hot water and beat till smooth. Bake 35 minutes.

NOTE: Always test for doneness! A toothpick or cake tester inserted must come out dry and clean. Listen to your cake. If there is any sizzling, put it back in for another minute or so. Gently press top with finger. If the depression remains, your cake will need another minute. If it springs back, good indication that it is done.

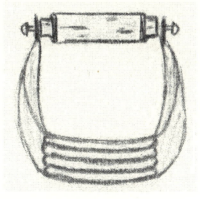

RHUBARB BREAD
Yield: 2 –9X5 LOAVES

This is a 5 star recipe to be sure – originally from my cousin Beatrice Oaks from Park River, North Dakota.

1 ½ cups firmly packed **brown sugar**
2/3 cup **liquid shortening**
1 cup **buttermilk** or **sour milk**
1 **egg**
1 teaspoon **vanilla**
2 ½ cups all-purpose **flour**
1 teaspoon **baking soda**
1 teaspoon **salt**
1 ½ cups chopped uncooked fresh **rhubarb**
½ cup chopped **nuts**, optional
½ cup granulated **sugar**
1 ½ tablespoons grated **orange peel**, optional
2 tablespoons **butter**, room temperature

Preheat oven to 325 degrees and grease two 9x5 inch loaf pans; line bottom and sides with waxed paper. Combine brown sugar and oil in large bowl and beat well. Mix buttermilk, egg and vanilla in a small bowl. Add to brown sugar mixture and blend thoroughly. Mix together the flour, soda and salt. Combine the wet and dry ingredients and fold in rhubarb and nuts. Divide batter evenly between prepared loaf pans. Combine sugar, orange peel and butter in small bowl and sprinkle over loaves. Bake until tester inserted in center of loaves comes out clean, about 1 hour. Let cool in pans 10 minutes, then turn out onto racks. Remove waxed paper when loaves are completely cool.

SCONES
Yield: 12 wedges

These are delicious! In fact, they are divine! Dad loved them with his afternoon tea.

2 cups all purpose **flour**
3 tablespoons **brown sugar**
2 teaspoons **baking powder**
½ teaspoon **salt**
¼ cup (1/2 stick) **butter**
1 8 ounce carton **sour cream**
1 beaten **egg yolk**
1 slightly beaten **egg white**

Stir together the flour, brown sugar, baking powder, and salt. Using a pastry blender cut in the butter. Make well in the center. In small bowl stir together the sour cream and the egg yolk. Add all at once to the flour mixture. Use a fork to combine. Turn on floured surface and knead 10 or 12 strokes. Pat into a 9 inch circle and cut in to 12 wedges. Place on an ungreased sheet about 1 inch apart and brush lightly with the egg white. Bake in a preheated 400 degree oven for 10 or 12 minutes.

VARIATION: Pour boiling water over ½ cup (or more) snipped dried sweet cherries or cranberries or raisins. Let stand 5 minutes. Drain well. Toss the fruit and 1 teaspoon finely shredded orange peel into the flour mixture before adding the sour cream mixture. Continue as directed.

SOUR CREAM COFFEE CAKE
Yield: 1 – 9x9 pan

There are many sour cream coffee cake recipes floating around, but you can't do much better than this one.

¼ pound **butter** or **margarine** (1 stick)
1 ½ cups granulated **sugar**
2 **eggs**, lightly beaten
1 teaspoon **baking soda**
1 cup **sour cream**
1 teaspoon **vanilla**
2 cups sifted all-purpose **flour**
1 ½ teaspoons **baking powder**

Streusel Mixture
½ cup **brown sugar**
¾ cup chopped **nuts**
1 teaspoon **cinnamon**

Preheat oven to 350 degrees and grease a 9x9x2 pan. Cream thoroughly the butter and the sugar. Add the eggs. Put soda in the sour cream and add to the batter. Add vanilla and dry ingredients. Place half the batter, the streusel mixture and then the other half of the batter in splotches in pan. Bake for 40-45 minutes.

NOTE: A tip I learned early on – if you don't grease the sides of your pan, you will have a higher cake!

SOUTHERN SPOON BREAD
Yield: 6 servings

This fluffy light spoon bread has a moist texture like a souffle. We often served this instead of potatoes. For a luncheon dish one could serve it with creamed chicken or seafood.

2 cups **milk**
½ cup **corn meal**
1 teaspoon **salt**
¼ teaspoon **baking powder**
3 **egg yolks**
2 tablespoons **butter**
3 **egg whites**

Preheat oven to 350 degrees and butter 1½ quart casserole. Scald milk; add corn meal and cook until mixture is very thick. Add salt and baking powder. Beat egg yolks until light. Add a small amount of the corn-meal mixture to the yolks and then combine both mixtures. Add butter and fold in egg whites beaten to soft peaks. Turn into casserole and bake uncovered for 25 to 30 minutes or until well puffed. Serve immediately in casserole for it quickly falls!

YEAST BREADS

I REMEMBER . . . bread baking was a weekly activity in our home. I'm not sure Mother baked on the same day every week, but she did bake bread regularly. I remember 2 or 3 large loaves of white bread and a gigantic pan of caramel rolls on the kitchen table. And I remember that the morning after Mother had baked bread, Daddy had thick slices with butter and Roquefort cheese for breakfast!

When I was little, I thought a slice of "bought" bread was a real treat and envied my friends who had it on a regular basis. As I grew older and my palette became more cultivated, I realized how fortunate we had been to have had a Mother who liked to bake. Any time we had company for an afternoon party or for dinner, fresh rolls were always featured.

Today Jeannie is our bread baker. She has introduced us to a wonderful combination of flours and seeds and berries. Her French peasant bread is without equal and her various kinds of bread sticks are addictive.

BASIC BREADSTICKS WITH VARIATIONS
Yield: 36 breadsticks

These are FANTASTIC! At several dinner parties we served a variety of breadsticks presented in a high crystal pitcher! Once again, thanks to Jeannie for this recipe and the presentation!

1 cup warm **water** (about 105 degrees)
¼ ounce package active **dry yeast**
3 cups unbleached all-purpose **flour**
2 teaspoons **salt**
5 tablespoons **extra-virgin olive oil, vegetable oil,** or **butter**
2 to 3 tablespoons **cornmeal** for dusting pans.

In a small bowl whisk together water and yeast. In another bowl combine flour and salt. Add oil or butter and beat until thoroughly combined. Add yeast mixture and beat until dough forms a ball, about 5 minutes. On a lightly floured surface knead dough just until it forms a smooth ball. Put dough in a lightly greased bowl and let rise, covered tightly until doubled in bulk, about 1 hour. On lightly floured surface knead dough lightly to deflate and form into a ball. Return dough to bowl, cover tightly with plastic wrap and chill at least 2 hours and up to 1 day. Preheat oven to 325 degrees and lightly dust 3 large baking sheets with cornmeal. Turn dough out onto a floured surface and pat dough into a 9 inch square and cut in half to form 2 rectangles. Cut each rectangle crosswise into 4 ½ by ½ inch strips for a total of 36 pieces. Roll and stretch each piece of dough with palms of hands to form a narrow stick 12 to 15 inches long. Arrange breadsticks as formed on pans about 1/2 inch apart and let rest 10 minutes. Bake 2 pans of breadsticks in upper and lower thirds of oven, switching their positions halfway through baking, until breadsticks are firm, crisp, and pale golden, 20 to 30 minutes. Transfer breadsticks to racks and cool.

NOTE: For added crunch, before baking, lightly brush with egg wash (beat 1 large egg white with 1 tablespoon water) and roll in sesame or poppy seeds.

WHOLE WHEAT WALNUT BREADSTICKS

Now here is a favorite variation on the theme!

2 ½ cups **all-purpose flour**
1 cup **warm water**
¼ ounce package **active dry yeast**
2/3 cup **whole-wheat flour**
2 teaspoons **salt**
4 tablespoons **oil**
½ cup finely **chopped walnuts**

Just follow the recipe for basic breadsticks, substituting above ingredients for basic breadstick dough ingredients. After first rising of dough, knead in nuts.

NOTE: In all the variations, if the dough seems too dry, feel free to add some more water. In Arizona this is often necessary.

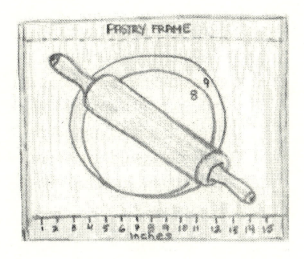

BUTTERSCOTCH STICKY BUNS
Yield: 24 buns

Don't let the length of this recipe discourage you. It will seem a simple and easy procedure after the first or second try. And you do remember how delicious they were, don't you?

½ cup **milk**
½ cup granulated **sugar**
1 teaspoon salt
2/3 cup **butter** or **margarine**
½ cup very warm **water**
2 envelopes active dry **yeast**
4 **eggs** beaten
4 ½ cups sifted all-purpose **flour**
½ cup softened **butter**, or a little more
2/3 cup granulated **sugar**
1 teaspoon **cinnamon**
1 cup **raisins** (optional)
Butterscotch Mixture
1 ½ cups firmly packed **brown sugar**
1 cup **light corn syrup**
½ cup **butter**
1 cup **walnut** or **pecan halves**

Combine milk, sugar, salt and butter or margarine in a saucepan. Heat just until butter/margarine is melted; cool to lukewarm. Sprinkle yeast into very warm water in a large bowl. (Very warm water should feel comfortably warm when dropped on wrist). Add lukewarm milk mixture, eggs and 2 cups of the flour; beat until smooth. Add just enough of the remaining flour to make a soft dough. Knead until smooth and elastic, about 5 minutes, using only as much flour as needed to keep dough from sticking. Place dough in a large greased bowl; turn the dough over to bring the greased side up. Cover. Let rise in warm place about 2 hours or until double in bulk. Punch down. Let rise again. (This second rising is rare in recipes these days. But I always let breads rise twice because I believe it makes a lighter, finer textured dough).

While dough is rising, prepare the butterscotch mixture: Combine the brown sugar, corn syrup and the butter in a saucepan; simmer for 2 minutes. Divide evenly into two 9x9x2 inch baking pans. Sprinkle with nuts. Divide dough in half and roll each piece to a 15x8 inch rectangle on a lightly floured pastry board. Spread with softened butter. Combine 2/3 cup granulated sugar and 1 teaspoon cinnamon and sprinkle half on each rectangle. Then, if you choose, sprinkle about ½ cup raisins on each rectangle. Roll up jelly roll fashion beginning with the long end and cut into 12 equal slices. Place them close together in the pans and let rise until double in bulk. Bake in a moderate oven (375 degrees) 25 minutes or until golden brown. Switch shelves half way through. Turn upside down on a large platter. Leave pan in place 5 minutes to allow topping to run over buns. Lift off pan.

JEANNIE'S FABULOUS FRENCH BREAD

Yield: 2 loaves

Lacking knowledge of the origin of this fine recipe we are not able to offer credit where credit is due, but Jeannie did make it a family favorite.

1 envelope active dry **yeast**
¼ cup warm **water** (110 degrees)
about 3 cups all-purpose **flour**
1 teaspoon **sugar**
1 teaspoon **salt**
1 to 1 ¼ cups ice-cold **water**

In a small bowl, sprinkle the yeast over the ¼ cup warm water. Let the mixture stand until it starts to bubble, about 10 minutes. Using an electric mixer and dough hook (or mixing by hand), mix 3 cups flour, sugar and salt in a large bowl. Add yeast mixture and 1 cup of the cold water. Beat on medium speed or with a heavy spoon until well-blended. Change to a dough hook or use a heavy spoon. Beat until dough is shiny, elastic and slightly sticky, about 5 minutes with mixer, 10 to 20 minutes by hand. If the dough is dry or difficult to beat, add more water, one or two teaspoons at a time. Let dough rise, covered with plastic wrap, in a warm place until it doubles in size, 1 ½ to 2 hours.

To shape the loaves, sprinkle about 2 tablespoons flour over dough and scrape out onto a well-floured board. Divide the dough in half. With floured hands, lightly pat each portion of dough into a 7x8 inch rectangle. Starting on a short side, roll dough jelly-roll fashion pressing the last exposed side to the loaf. Let loaves rest, lightly covered with plastic wrap, on the board for 30 minutes. Carefully pick up ends of each loaf and transfer to a greased or cooking parchment-lined 14x17 inch baking sheet. In the move stretch each loaf to a length of 12 to 14 inches. (If loaf sticks to board, gently scrape free with a spatula). Place loaves 4 to 5 inches apart. Cover loosely with plastic wrap; let rise in a warm place until loaves are slightly puffy, 10 to 15 minutes. Pre-heat oven to 475 degrees. Put bread sheet on the middle shelf and immediately turn heat down to 425 degrees. Spray every 10 minutes with ice water. Bake until golden brown all over, 20 to 30 minutes.

NOTE: Jeannie pours a cup or so of water directly on the oven floor prior to baking and removes bread from sheet onto oven shelf about 10 minutes before they are done.

OATMEAL BREAD

Yield: 2 large loaves

I made this bread often when you children were growing up. It is really delicious!

1 cup quick **oatmeal**
2 cups boiling **water**
1 teaspoon **salt**
¼ cup granulated **sugar**
2 tablespoons **shortening**, melted
4 tablespoons molasses
1 package **yeast**
½ cup lukewarm **water**
1 teaspoon **sugar**
6 cups all-purpose **flour**

Scald oatmeal with the boiling water; add salt, sugar, shortening and molasses. Dissolve yeast in lukewarm water to which one teaspoon sugar has been added. Add yeast and flour 1 cup at a time, to make workable dough. Knead and let rise until double in bulk. Punch down and let rise again. When double in bulk, punch down, make into loaves and let rise until double again. Preheat oven to 350 degrees and bake until nicely brown and until it sounds hollow when tapped with your fingers – about 30 or 40 minutes. Remove immediately from the pans and let cool on a wire rack.

ORANGE ROLLS
Yield: 15 rolls

This is an old-fashioned recipe, one might say, but too good to omit. Delicious for breakfast or served with a salad for lunch —they are not overly sweet.

1 cup **milk**
3 tablespoons **butter**
3 **eggs**
½ cup granulated **sugar**
1 package dry **yeast**
1 teaspoon **salt**
4 cups all-purpose **flour**
½ cup softened **butter**
½ cup granulated **sugar**
grated **rind of 1 orange**

Scald milk and add 3 tablespoons butter. Beat eggs slightly and then add the sugar. When the milk is lukewarm, add yeast and salt. Add the milk and yeast to the egg mixture and mix well. Add 1 cup flour and beat. Let rise 2 hours. Add 3 cups flour to the sponge. Stir but do not knead at any time. Let rise 2 hours longer. On a floured surface, roll into a rectangle and spread with the ½ cup softened butter, ½ cup sugar and the grated rind of 1 orange. Roll and cut as for cinnamon rolls. Let rise in greased muffin tins for 2 hours. Preheat oven to 375 degrees and bake for 15 – 20 minutes. Remove immediately from tins and cool on a wire rack.

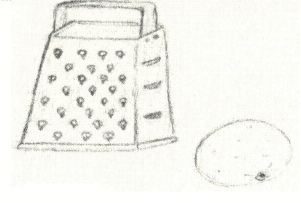

DESSERTS

I REMEMBER . . . how much my Dad loved pie and what good crust my Mother made. She always baked the "scraps" with cinnamon and sugar for us.

I hope you won't be turned off by the length of the recipe for Grandma Everson's apple pie, but I thought it was important to record the procedure, every step of the way.

In this day and age, we rarely serve pie for dessert. More often we end our company meals with frozen or refrigerated sweets. And in this category Jeannie thinks we have some of the best recipes around.

APPLE CRISP

Yield: 9 servings

Apple Crisp has always been a favorite and easy dessert. There are many variations on this theme, but this is the version we concocted.

8 – 10 medium sized pie **apples** (tart, that is)
¾ cup granulated **sugar**
¼ cup **water**
½ cup **butter**
1 cup **brown sugar**
1 cup all-purpose **flour**
½ teaspoon **baking powder**
½ teaspoon **salt**

Preheat oven to 375 degrees and grease a 9x9 inch pan. Cover the bottom of the pan with peeled, sliced apples. Sprinkle first with the granulated sugar, then the water. Mix butter, brown sugar, flour, baking powder and salt until it is crumbly. You can use your finger tips for this. Sprinkle this mixture over the top of the apples. Bake for 35 – 40 minutes or until apples are tender and the top is brown. Serve warm with real whipped cream or vanilla ice cream.

CUSTARD

Yield: 4 – 5 servings

This is an old recipe but a good one. And so simple. Check for doneness by inserting a silver knife about 1 inch in from the edge. If it comes out clean, it's done! This is excellent "invalid" food. We used to make this a lot for Daddy when he was sick.

4 **eggs**
1 quart **milk**
½ cup granulated **sugar**

Slightly beat the eggs. Add milk and sugar. Pour into the top of a double boiler and sprinkle with nutmeg. Steam for 20 minutes or until set. Covered!

CREAM PUFFS
Yield: 10 large puffs

If you remember, these were so popular in our home that sometimes we had them instead of birthday cakes!

Puffs
½ cup **butter**
1 cup boiling **water**
1 cup sifted all-purpose **flour**
¼ teaspoon **salt**
4 **eggs**, unbeaten

Preheat oven to 450 degrees. Combine butter and water in a medium sized saucepan and bring to boil. Add flour and salt all at once and stir constantly until mixture leaves sides of pan in a smooth compact shiny mass. Remove from heat and cool slightly. At this point I usually put the batter in a medium sized bowl and use the electric beater. Add the eggs, one at a time, beating thoroughly after each addition. Beat steadily until mixture is smooth and satiny. Drop from tablespoon 2 inches apart on ungreased cookie sheet. Bake for 10 to 15 minutes. Reduce heat to 350 degrees and bake 20 minutes longer. At this point make a small slit on the side of each puff with a sharp knife and continue to bake for 5 minutes or until golden brown. (The slit allows the center to dry out a bit, and this is what you want.)

Cream Puff Filling
1 cup **milk**
½ cup granulated **sugar**
¼ teaspoon **salt**
3 tablespoons all-purpose **flour**
½ cup **milk**
2 **eggs**
1 tablespoon **butter**
1 teaspoon **vanilla**
1 cup **heavy cream**, whipped

Scald the 1 cup milk in double boiler. Mix dry ingredients and then add the remaining ½ cup of milk to the dry ingredients and mix to a smooth paste. Pour this mixture into the hot milk and stir slowly until thick, 5 to 8 minutes. Beat the eggs. Add some hot mixture slowly to the beaten eggs and return to the double boiler, cooking 3 to 5 minutes longer. Add butter and vanilla. Cool completely. When cold, beat again, fold in the whipped cream and fill the puffs.

Chocolate Glaze
2 tablespoons **butter**
2 squares **unsweetened chocolate**
3 tablespoons **hot milk**
1 cup **confectioners' sugar**
½ teaspoon **salt**

Heat butter and chocolate in double boiler until melted. Combine milk, confectioner's sugar and salt. Add to chocolate mixture gradually, stirring until smooth.

TO ASSEMBLE: When the puffs are cool, cut off tops, remove any moist pieces of puff, fill with custard, replace top and drop a tablespoon or so of chocolate glaze on the "hat."

CREAM PIE FILLING
Yield: 8 servings

This is the same recipe that I use for the cream puffs. Versatile, don't you think?

1 cup **milk**
2 **eggs**
½ cup granulated **sugar**
1 tablespoon **butter**
¼ teaspoon **salt**
1 teaspoon **vanilla**
3 tablespoons **flour**
1 cup **heavy cream**, whipped
½ cup **milk**
1 – 9 inch **baked pie shell**

Scald the 1 cup of milk in a double boiler. Mix dry ingredients. Add the remaining ½ cup of milk to the dry ingredients and stir until it is a smooth paste. Pour paste into the hot milk stirring slowly until thick, 5 – 8 minutes. Beat the eggs. Add some of the hot mixture slowly into the beaten eggs and return it to the double boiler, cooking 3 to 5 minutes longer. (If you added the eggs directly to the hot mixture, instead of the other way around, your custard would curdle.) Add the butter and vanilla. Cool thoroughly. Put in a baked 9 inch pie shell using one of the variations:

Banana: Use four ripe bananas. Fill pastry shell with alternate layers of sliced bananas and cooled filling.

Chocolate: Add 2 ounces melted chocolate and ¼ cup granulated sugar before adding hot mixture to egg in filling.

Spread whipped cream on pie. (If you would like a fluffier pie stir the whipped cream into the filling. For a spectacular pie, garnish with even more whipped cream - John's idea of heaven).

ENGLISH PLUM PUDDING
Yield: 12-16 servings

This was Grandma Everson's recipe – we had it in our home every Thanksgiving and every Christmas. It is a wonderful old recipe – and – I'm sure you remember – the sauce is magnificent!

Pudding
½ cup **molasses**
½ cup **corn syrup**
1 cup chopped **suet**
¼ cup **citron**
1 pound **dates**, chopped
1 cup **sweet milk**
1 cup chopped **walnuts**
2 ½ cups all-purpose **flour**
1 teaspoon **baking soda**
1 teaspoon **salt**

Mix all of the ingredients in the order given and pour into a buttered oven-proof dish or mold with a secure cover. Put a rack in a large pot, adding enough water to reach the rack. Place the mold on the rack and steam for about 2 ½ hours. Check often and add more water if necessary. This will keep for many months and can be reheated by steaming.

Sauce
½ cup **butter**
1 cup granulated **sugar**
½ cup **heavy cream**
2 **egg yolks**
2 **egg whites**, beaten stiff

Cream together the butter and sugar. Gently beat the egg yolks with the cream and add to the mixture. Put it all in the top of a double boiler and cook for about 5 minutes. Turn down the heat and keep warm until serving time. When ready to serve, gently fold in the beaten egg whites.

GRANDMA EVERSON'S APPLE PIE
Yield: 1 – 9 inch pie

When I was a child, I remember that Mother always used pure lard in her pie crusts – and they were always light and flaky. She always told me that one should work as quickly as possible with crust – the less it is handled the better. As I recall, she pretty much used 2 cups of all-purpose flour to 1 cup of lard, salt and the least amount of ice water that will hold it together. As the years went by, I noticed that she turned to crisco or any homogenized shortening – in about the same proportions. When I began to bake, I experimented some and decided that the proportions should be 2 cups of flour to 2/3 cup plus 1 tablespoon shortening. Salt and ice water as usual. I decided to use either butter or margarine instead of crisco. But the secret to good crust remains the same – work as quickly as possible!

I think Grandma was the only person in the world who did not add 2 tablespoons of flour to the sugar mixture. This meant, of course, that there was quite a lot of juice when the pie was piping hot – but we always preferred that to a thickened filling.

Crust
2 cups all-purpose **flour**
2/3 cup plus 1 tablespoon **butter or margarine**
2 teaspoons **salt**
4 – 5 tablespoons **ice water**

Mix the flour, butter and salt together until it is crumbly. Add water gradually, just enough to hold it together. Divide dough in half. Roll out bottom crust, put it in the pie pan and refrigerate while you prepare the apples. Form the remaining dough into a ball and refrigerate as well.

NOTE: In rolling pastry, it's best to use a pastry cloth. Rub flour well into the cloth, and brush off the excess. Roll pastry from center out, using light strokes and alternating direction to form an even circle.

Filling

7 cups of peeled and thinly sliced **apples** (2 ½ pounds more or less). What you want to do is pile them high in the crust and always try to use a tart cooking apple.

1 – 1 ½ cups of **granulated sugar** (depending on the tartness of the apples)
1 tablespoon freshly squeezed **lemon juice**
1 teaspoon **nutmeg**
½ teaspoon **salt**
4 ounces (1/2 stick) **butter**

Toss the peeled and sliced apples with the lemon juice and the mixture of sugar, nutmeg and salt. Pile into the pie shell. Dot the apples with the butter cut into small pieces. Put the pie pan in the refrigerator while you prepare the top crust.

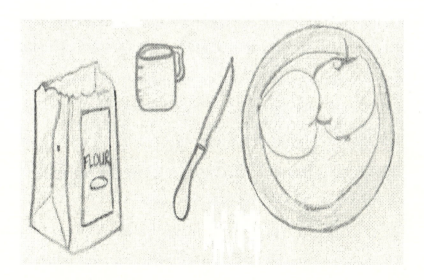

Top Crust

Roll out, as you did with the bottom crust and cut slits for steam vents. Carefully place folded pastry over the filling. Trim overhanging edge of pastry so it measures 1 inch from edge all around. Moisten the edge of the bottom pastry with a little water and fold top pastry under edge of bottom pastry. With fingers, press edge together to seal so juices won't run out. Crimp edge: Place thumb on edge of pastry at an angle. Pinch dough between index finger and thumb. Repeat at same angle all around pie. Place in preheated 425 degree oven. After 15 minutes or so, turn down the temperature to 375 degrees. Bake an additional 45 to 50 minutes, or until apples are fork-tender and crust is golden. 10 to 15 minutes before removing the pie, brush the crust with a mixture of 2 tablespoons milk and 2 tablespoons granulated sugar. Return to oven. This addition makes a nice glaze - the finishing touch! Serve warm.

ICE CREAM CLAD IN CHOCOLATE
Yield: 16 servings

Children – this is a sensational party dessert and really very simple to make. I made this several times in Bucks County (I still make it) and it always received rave reviews!

4 cups **chocolate wafer crumbs** (two 8 ½ ounce boxes – found in most super markets)
1 cup melted **butter**
1 quart **vanilla ice cream**, slightly softened
1 quart **pistachio ice cream**, slightly softened
1 quart **chocolate ice cream**, slightly softened
(or any other combination of flavors that you choose)

Make crumbs from chocolate wafers in the blender or with a rolling pin. Just be sure they are very fine. Combine the crumbs with the melted butter; then set aside 2/3 cup of these crumbs. Firmly press remaining crumbs over the bottom and sides of a 9 inch spring form pan, having round bottom insert in place. Freeze about 15 minutes or until firm. Remove from freezer and quickly spread vanilla ice cream over bottom in even layer. Sprinkle with 1/3 cup reserved crumbs. Return to freezer until ice cream is firm. Repeat step 5, using pistachio ice cream. Carefully spread second quart of ice cream, sprinkle with crumbs, and return to freezer until icecream is firm. Proceed with the third quart of icecream (no crumbs on top). Cover top of pan with foil and return to freezer until needed. About 10 minutes before serving, invert spring form pan onto chilled serving plate – a large crystal plate would be lovely! Garnish using your creative spirit!

NEVER FAIL MERINGUE TORTE
Yield: 8 servings

Now, this shell is the beginning of any number of wonderful desserts. It can be filled with any kind of fresh fruit and then topped with lots of real whipped cream. Or you can make a lemon filling and have what we have always called Angel Pie. The recipe for that is below.

Meringue

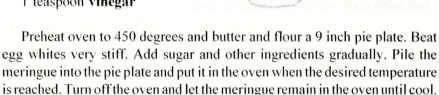

4 **egg whites**
1 1/3 cups **granulated sugar**
½ teaspoon **salt**
2 teaspoons **cornstarch**
1 teaspoon **vinegar**

Preheat oven to 450 degrees and butter and flour a 9 inch pie plate. Beat egg whites very stiff. Add sugar and other ingredients gradually. Pile the meringue into the pie plate and put it in the oven when the desired temperature is reached. Turn off the oven and let the meringue remain in the oven until cool.

Lemon Custard Filling

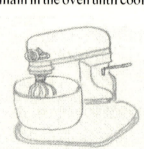

4 **egg yolks**
½ cup **granulated sugar**
2 tablespoons grated **lemon rind**
1 cup **heavy cream**
4 tablespoons freshly squeezed **lemon juice**

Beat 4 egg yolks until thick and lemon-colored. Gradually beat in the ½ cup granulated sugar Blend in the lemon juice and the grated lemon rind. Cook over hot water, stirring constantly, until thick (5 to 8 minutes). Cool thoroughly. Whip until stiff the 1 cup heavy cream. Fold in 2 tablespoons granulated or confectioner's sugar and 1 teaspoon vanilla. Beat the cooled custard to lighten it. Then mix gently ½ of the cream into the custard. Spread the custard on the meringue shell and top with remaining cream. Chill about 12 hours before serving.

OLD FASHIONED BREAD PUDDING
Yield: 6 – 8 servings

A recipe from Springfield – Church of the Redeemer Cookbook – submitted by our friend Betty Keating. This is certainly a delectable way to use "stale" bread!

6 slices **toast**, buttered (good French or Italian bread is best)
3 **eggs** beaten
½ cup **granulated sugar**
¼ teaspoon **salt**
3 cups warm **milk**
2 teaspoons **vanilla**
6 teaspoons **granulated sugar**
2 teaspoons **cinnamon**

Preheat oven to 350 degrees and grease a 9x9 inch baking dish. Put quartered slices of buttered toast into dish. Mix together eggs, sugar, salt, milk and vanilla and pour it over the toast. Let stand 10 minutes and then sprinkle with mixture of sugar and cinnamon. Bake for about 30 minutes or until set.

NOTE: Remember the test – put a silver knife into the custard about 1 inch from edge. If it comes out clean, it's "set!"

PUMPKIN FLAN

Yield: 12 servings

This is a spectacular dessert! Through the years we seemed to prefer this to the old-fashioned pumpkin pie with crust.

1 ¼ cups **granulated sugar**
3 cups **light cream**, scalded
2 cups **canned pumpkin**
2/3 cup **granulated sugar**
6 whole **eggs** plus 2 **egg yolks**, slightly beaten
1 teaspoon each **salt** and **cinnamon**
¼ teaspoon **ginger**
½ teaspoon **nutmeg**
1 cup **heavy cream**
1 tablespoon **confectioner's sugar**
1 teaspoon **vanilla**

Slowly melt 1 ¼ cups sugar in a heavy frying pan, stirring until it becomes a smooth deep amber syrup. Pour into a well-chilled, round-bottomed heat resistant 2 quart glass casserole. Tip to coat sides and bottom of bowl. Chill while you prepare custard. Mix well all remaining ingredients, except the heavy cream, confectioners' sugar and vanilla, and pour into the caramel-lined bowl. Set bowl in a pan of hot water and bake in a preheated 350 degree oven for about 1 ¼ hours or until set. Test by putting a silver knife into the custard about 1 inch from the edge. If it comes out clean, it's done. It's "set!" Cool at room temperature for 30 minutes and then invert on serving plate. After 10 minutes lift off the bowl. In a chilled 1 quart bowl whip the 1 cup of heavy cream until it forms soft peaks. Stir in 1 tablespoon confectioner's sugar and 1 teaspoon vanilla. Place a dollop on each serving.

RHUBARB PIE
Yield: 8 servings

How can this be so very, very good when it is so very, very easy?

4 cups cut up fresh **rhubarb**
1 cup **granulated sugar**
6 **soda crackers**, crushed
3 **eggs**, slightly beaten
2 tablespoons **water**
1 – 9 inch **pie crust**

Preheat oven to 400 degrees. Fill pie shell with rhubarb and pour over a mixture of sugar, crackers, beaten eggs and water. Bake for 15 minutes and then lower temperature to 325 degrees until custard is set. Put a silver knife in the custard, half-way between the edge and the center. If it comes out clean, it is set! Serve warm with whipped cream or vanilla ice cream.

VARIATION: Omit the crust and bake in a greased 9x9 inch pan at 325 degrees.

RASPBERRY BOMBE

Yield: 12 servings

This is one of the prettiest desserts I know – lovely in the spring, although our friend Kenny Seidel asked for the recipe because she wanted to serve it for Christmas Dinner!

The Bombe

1 cup **heavy cream**, whipped
½ cup **chopped walnuts**
¼ cup chopped **maraschino cherries**
1 cup sifted **confectioners' sugar**
2 teaspoons **vanilla**
1 quart **raspberry sherbet**

Gently fold together the first five ingredients. Line a 1 ½ quart mold with a thick layer of the mixture. Fill the large hollow in the center with slightly softened raspberry sherbet. Cover it smoothly with the rest of the cream mixture. Cover it all with a sheet of waxed paper and a tight fitting lid. Place in the freezer for at least 3 hours. (It will, of course, last for a long time in the freezer – a very good make-ahead dessert!)

The Sauce

1 (10 ounce) box **frozen raspberries**
2 tablespoons **water**
¼ cup **granulated sugar**
1 teaspoon **lemon juice**

Boil the raspberries, water and the sugar gently for 4 minutes. Force the mixture through a fine sieve into a jar – being very careful not to force so hard that you get seeds – it should be seedless! Add lemon juice. Cover and chill in the refrigerator. (This too can be made many days in advance of serving.)

Serve: Remove the lid and place the bombe in a pan of hot water for a moment. Turn upside down on a beautiful crystal dessert platter and surround with the sauce.

TEMPERANCE MINCEMEAT
Yield: Filling for 20 pies

Now I don't suppose you will ever cook in such quantities, but I felt constrained to include this recipe because it was one that I grew up with – my mother made this every winter. Mincemeat was one of my dad's favorite pies. Sometimes, however, he ate more than he should and suffered from a little "heart-burn" as a result!

3 pints finely **chopped beef** (ground round)
5 pints finely chopped **apples**, peeled
1 cup finely **chopped suet**
4 pints **granulated sugar**
1 pint **molasses**
1 pint **vinegar**
2 pints **water**
2 pints **currants**
1 pint **chopped raisins**
1 pint **whole raisins**
1 tablespoon **salt**
2 tablespoons **cinnamon**
1 tablespoon **cloves**
1 tablespoon **allspice**
1 tablespoon freshly grated **nutmeg**

Mix well and boil gently until the apples are tender. My Mother always preserved the mincemeat in Mason jars. Today I guess we would freeze it in pie containers.

SLICED ORANGES WITH ORANGE CREAM

Yield: 10 servings

This is a lovely dessert — pretty and delicious and refreshing. A clear glass serving dish enhances the presentation.

1 ¼ cups strained **fresh orange juice**
6 -8 large **navel oranges**
grated **rind** of 2 **navel oranges**
5 **egg yolks**
1 cup **granulated sugar**
½ pint **heavy cream**

Prepare 1 ¼ cups freshly squeezed, strained orange juice. Grate the rind of 2 navel oranges and add immediately to the juice. Peel oranges. After removing as much pith as possible, slice in thin rounds. Place in a serving dish and refrigerate until ready to serve. In a medium bowl beat the yolks of 5 eggs until thick and pale with a rotary beater, preferably electric. Gradually beat in 1 cup granulated sugar. Stir in the strained orange juice. Place mixture in the top of a 2 quart enamel double boiler over boiling water and cook, beating constantly with a rotary beater until it foams up and is well thickened, about 4 minutes. Remove from burner and cool. When cold, refrigerate until ready to serve. Just before serving, beat ½ pint heavy cream until stiff and fold it carefully into the orange sauce. Pour it over the sliced oranges and serve at once – with or without angel or sponge cake or lady fingers.

STAINED GLASS ICE
Yield: 12 servings

Another make-ahead. Good for a crowd. Really easy! And pretty! And delicious! This recipe came from Jean Duncan, one of Dad's secretaries at St. Martin's Church.

4 pints **sherbet** (4 different flavors if you can get them)
1 pint **heavy cream**, whipped
¼ cup **granulated sugar**

Scoop sherbet into medium size balls (five from each pint) and put them in the freezer. Whip the cream until it is stiff and sweeten lightly with the ¼ cup sugar. Spoon four heaping tablespoons whipped cream into a large chilled angel food cake pan and place four balls of sherbet, one of each color, between the spoons of cream. Make additional layers, alternating sherbet and whipped cream. Continue quickly till all has been used. Press down with back of a spoon so the cream fills any spaces. Cover with plastic wrap; place in freezer overnight, or for many days. Unmold.

TARTE TATIN
Yield: 8 servings

The secret for this distinct and delicious tart, or so the story goes, was held by the Tatin sisters, who ran a small inn near Paris, and then by Maxim's, who obtained the recipe, they say, by sending one of its pastry chefs, disguised as a gardener, to spy on the Tatin establishment. But no secret can be kept forever – I discovered this recipe years ago while we were in Solebury. Absolutely wonderful!

Pastry

1 cup **all-purpose flour**
1/3 cup plus 1 tablespoon **butter**
1 teaspoon **salt**
2 – 3 tablespoons **ice water**

Mix the flour, butter and salt until crumbly, using finger tips. Handle as little as possible. Work quickly. Add 1 tablespoon of water at a time, using just enough to hold it together. Form into a ball and refrigerate it until ready to assemble.

The Filling

¼ pound **sweet butter**
1 cup **granulated sugar**
4 – 5 large tart **cooking apples**, peeled and sliced
½ pint **heavy cream**, whipped

Preheat oven to 450 degrees and coat the sides and bottom of a 9 inch pie plate with butter (for best results use heavy porcelain ironwear or other heavy pan). Cover the butter completely with ½ inch of sugar. Place in refrigerator while you peel and slice the apples. Fill the chilled pan to the brim with apple slices and top with the remaining butter and sugar. Roll pastry – 1/8 inch thick. Cover the apples but do not seal. Bake for 25 to 30 minutes. Check occasionally to see that the apples are not cooking too fast. They should be a light golden brown and the sugar should caramelize.

Place an oven-proof plate over the cooked pie and invert. It may spread a little, but that's all right. Sprinkle with a little more sugar and place directly under the broiler for 2 or 3 minutes. Serve warm with a dollop of whipped cream, lightly sweetened and with 1 teaspoon vanilla.

COOKIES

I REMEMBER . . . when I was a little girl, I mean five or six years old, I used to ask my friends' mothers for recipes, especially recipes for cookies. The mothers in our neighborhood were very good about providing afternoon snacks! When I brought the recipes home, mother let me make them, and without much supervision as I recall.

Actually I remember that one day when mother was at Ladies Aid, I decided to make doughnuts – and I was in the fourth grade! The amazing thing is that the project was accomplished without any serious accidents – no fires, no burns from hot grease. The end of the story is that I took a plate to my neighbor, Mrs. Acker. Her cleaning lady was there and she asked me if she could buy a dozen. I charged her 15 cents!

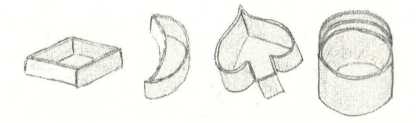

BUTTERSCOTCH BARS
Yield: 16 bars

Another super easy recipe. Chewy and delicious!

¼ pound (1 stick) **butter**
1 cup **brown sugar**, firmly packed
1 **egg yolk**
½ cup **flour**
1 teaspoon **baking powder**
1 teaspoon **vanilla**
1 cup **chopped nuts or dates**

Preheat oven to 350 degrees and grease a 9x9 pan. Heat butter and sugar until the butter is melted and the sugar is dissolved. Cool slightly. Add egg yolk and beat well. Add sifted flour and baking powder to sugar and butter syrup. Stir in vanilla and nuts or dates. Pour into pan and bake for 30 minutes. Cut immediately into bars.

CARAMEL GRAHAM CRACKER COOKIES

Yield: 48 single squares

You both know your mother's weakness for anything "caramel." When I first tasted this cookie 35 years ago at an EYC picnic in Springfield, I thought they were wonderful. Although I haven't made them much through the years, it is a recipe that should be kept and used every now and again when you are short on time. Did I say it is easy? It's easy!

24 double **graham cracker squares**
½ pound **butter**
1 cup **brown sugar**, firmly packed
1 ½ cup **chopped walnuts or pecans** (6 ounces)

Preheat oven to 350 degrees. Place all the graham crackers on an ungreased large rimmed baking sheet – you will need two I'm sure. In a small heavy saucepan over moderate heat, melt butter and brown sugar. Bring to a boil and stir constantly while boiling for 5 minutes. Pour caramelized mixture evenly over the graham crackers. Sprinkle top with nuts. Bake 10 minutes and then cool 10 minutes in the pan. Remove carefully and put on brown paper to continue to cool. Break them carefully into single squares. These may be frozen.

CINNAMON RAISIN BARS

Yield: 2 ½ dozen bars

This recipe is from a young adult at Holy Trinity. She said that one can freeze the bars after baking, and then ice them just before serving.

Preheat oven to 350 degrees and grease a 13x9x2 inch baking dish.

Cookie Crust

½ cup **butter**
1 cup **brown sugar**
1 ½ cups sifted **all-purpose flour**
½ teaspoon **baking soda**
½ teaspoon **salt**
1 ½ cups **quick-cooking rolled oats**
2 tablespoons **water**

Cream butter and sugar. Sift together flour, soda and salt and stir into creamed mixture. Add oats and 1 tablespoon water and mix until crumbly. Firmly pat half the mixture in baking dish. Add 1 tablespoon water to remaining mixture and set aside.

Raisin Filling

¼ cup **granulated sugar**
1 tablespoon **cornstarch**
1 cup **water**
2 cups **raisins**

Combine sugar, cornstarch and water in a small saucepan. Add raisins and cook over medium heat till thickened and bubbly. Spread filling into prepared crust. Distribute reserved oat mixture over filling and pat smooth. Bake about 35 minutes, until golden brown. Cool on rack. Combine 1 cup sifted confectioners' sugar, ¼ teaspoon ground cinnamon and about 1 tablespoon milk and drizzle over bars.

GINGER ALMOND BISCOTTI
Yield: about 30 biscotti

It is just in the last few years that we have become addicted to Biscotti. This variety is simply delicious!

¾ cup whole **almonds with skins**
½ teaspoon **salt**
½ cup **crystallized ginger**
¼ teaspoon **baking soda**
1 cup **all-purpose flour**
1 large **egg**
1½ cup **granulated sugar**
1 large **egg white**
1½ teaspoons **ground ginger**
½ teaspoon **vanilla**

Preheat oven to 300 degrees and grease a cookie sheet. In a shallow baking pan toast almonds in middle of oven until a shade darker, about 10 minutes. Cool. Very coarsely chop the nuts and the crystallized ginger. Into a bowl sift together flour, sugar, ground ginger, salt, and baking soda. In another bowl with an electric mixer beat together whole egg, egg white and vanilla. Stir in flour mixture and beat until combined well. Stir in almonds and crystallized ginger. Turn dough out onto floured board and knead 7 times. Shape into a 16 inch roll, place on baking sheet and flatten to 1 inch thick. Bake in middle of oven until pale golden, about 45 minutes. Turn loaf out onto a rack and cool 10 minutes. On a cutting board with a serrated knife cut loaf diagonally into 1/2 inch thick slices. Arrange biscotti on a baking sheet and bake in middle of oven until crisp, about 15 minutes. Turn over half way through baking time. Cool on rack.

GINGER SNAPS
Yield: 3 dozen

There are indeed lots of recipes for Ginger Snaps but this one calls for FRESHLY GRATED GINGER. Herein lies the secret of this delicious cookie.

¾ cup **butter**
1 cup **granulated sugar**
¼ cup **dark molasses**
1 **egg**, beaten
2 cups sifted **all-purpose flour**
1 teaspoon **cinnamon**
½ teaspoon **cloves**
1 teaspoon **baking soda**
½ teaspoon **salt**
1 HEAPING tablespoon **freshly grated ginger**

Cream thoroughly the butter and the sugar. Add the molasses and the egg. Add all the dry ingredients and mix well. Chill for 2 - 4 hours. When ready to bake, preheat the oven to 350 degrees and lightly grease cookie sheets. Form small amounts of dough into balls and then roll in granulated sugar. Place on cookie sheets with ample room between each. They do spread! Bake about 15 minutes and cool on brown paper.

NOTE: I have discovered that freezing the fresh ginger works well for this recipe. Simply peel and grate.

GINGERBREAD MEN AND WOMEN
Yield: 3 dozen

Remember how many times we made and decorated these little people? My goodness, it was fun!

½ cup **shortening**
½ cup **granulated sugar**
½ cup **molasses**
1 teaspoon **baking soda**
1 tablespoon **hot water**
2 ½ cups **all-purpose flour**
1 ½ teaspoons **cinnamon**
1 ½ teaspoons **ginger**
½ teaspoon **salt**

Preheat oven to 350 degrees and lightly grease cookie sheets. Melt shortening over low heat. Remove and cool. Blend in ½ cup sugar and ½ cup molasses. Add 1 teaspoon soda dissolved in 1 tablespoon hot water. Sift the flour and add the cinnamon, ginger and salt. Add to the first mixture and chill. Roll out as thin or as thick as you like and then use your cutters. Place on the sheets and bake 8 – 10 minutes. Decorate your people – skirts and pants and buttons and bows using several different colors. (Your standard food coloring does the trick.)

Note: Mix confectioners' sugar with enough milk (1 or 2 tablespoons per cup of sugar) to a consistency that can be used in your decorator equipment.

GREAT GRANDMOTHER EVENSON'S DOUGHNUTS

Yield: 3 dozen

This is an old fashioned recipe to be sure. But a good one! When we were children, Mother used to fry the "holes" for us. Did we ever love those! The doughnuts and the "holes" were usually sprinkled with confectioners' sugar!

2 **eggs**
1 cup **granulated sugar**
4 tablespoons melted **shortening**
1 cup **sour milk**
1 ½ teaspoons **baking soda**
4 cups sifted **all-purpose flour**
1 teaspoon **salt**

Melt shortening 4 to 6 inches deep in a heavy kettle. In a large bowl beat the eggs and gradually add the sugar. Add the melted shortening and the sour milk. Mix the soda and salt with the sifted flour and gently incorporate into the egg mixture. Roll out on a floured pastry cloth to about ½ inch thick. Cut with doughnut cutter and fry in hot grease. It is very important to turn each one as soon as it rises to the top. Turn only once more! Drain on paper towels.

NOTE: Now this is a little tricky. If the grease is not hot enough, the doughnuts will absorb too much grease. On the other hand, if it is too hot, it will brown too fast and leave you with a raw center. Test it by dropping a small piece of bread into the lard. If it sizzles and quickly browns, then it is about right.

MARGE'S OATMEAL COOKIES
Yield: 4 dozen

This recipe is from Marjorie Peterson, our neighbor and friend in Longport. My goodness, but they are good!

4 cups quick **oatmeal**
3 cups **brown sugar**
1 **egg**, beaten
½ teaspoon **salt**
½ pound (two sticks) **butter**, melted
1 teaspoon **vanilla**

Preheat oven to 350 degrees. Mix all ingredients thoroughly. Place about a tablespoon full on a lightly greased cookie sheet about 2 ½ inches apart. Bake for about 10 minutes or until nicely browned. Cool on brown paper.

LEBKUCHEN

Yield: 3 dozen

Throw away any other Lebkuchen recipe that you might have – this one is perfect! It came from Hazel Porter, an old friend of Dad's. It may not be the most beautiful cookie, but there is no doubt about it – it is delicious! You may want to add a touch of decoration on each one immediately after you have glazed it – perhaps a slice of green or red cherry, for it is, after all, considered a Christmas cookie!

Cookie Dough

½ cup **honey**
½ cup **molasses**
¾ cup **brown sugar**, packed
1 **egg**
1 teaspoon **allspice**
1 tablespoon **lemon juice**
1 teaspoon **grated lemon rind**
2 ¾ cups sifted **all-purpose flour**
½ teaspoon **baking soda**
teaspoon **cinnamon**
1 teaspoon **cloves**
1 teaspoon **nutmeg**
¾ cup cut up **citron**
¾ cup **chopped nuts**

Mix and bring to a boil the honey and the molasses. Cool thoroughly and stir in the brown sugar, egg, lemon juice and lemon rind. Sift together and stir in the flour, soda, cinnamon, cloves, allspice and nutmeg. Mix in the citron and nuts and chill overnight. Preheat oven to 350 degrees and make the icing. Directions on next page. Roll small amount of the dough at a time, keeping the rest chilled. Roll out ¼ inch thick and cut into oblongs, 1 ½ x 2 ½ inches. Place one inch apart on an ungreased baking sheet. Bake until when touched lightly, no imprint remains. This should take from 10 to 12 minutes. Brush the warm icing over the cookies the minute they are out of the oven. Cool and store to mellow.

Icing

1 cup **granulated sugar**
½ cup **water**
¼ cup **confectioners' sugar**

Boil together the granulated sugar and water until the first indication of a thread appears (230 degrees). Remove from heat and stir in the confectioners' sugar. When icing gets sugary, reheat slightly, adding a little water until clear again.

NOTE: To mellow cookies, store in an airtight container for a few days. Add a cut orange or apple changing it frequently to ensure freshness.

EXCELLENT SOFT OATMEAL COOKIES

Yield: 4 dozen

This recipe came from my good friend, Mary Ann Lindem. No, actually from her mother who was wonderful in the kitchen. These cookies are exactly as described – excellent and soft!

½ cup **butter or margarine**
1¾ cups **all-purpose flour**
1 cup **brown sugar**, firmly packed
½ teaspoon **baking powder**
2 **eggs**, well-beaten
½ teaspoon **baking soda**
1 ½ cups **dates**
¼ teaspoon **salt**
1 medium-sized **red apple**
½ teaspoon **vanilla**
1 cup **walnuts**
½ teaspoon **lemon extract**
½ cup **old-fashioned oatmeal**

Preheat the oven to 375 degrees and lightly grease cookie sheets. Cream the butter and the sugar. Add the eggs. Grind the dates, apple, walnuts and oatmeal and add to the creamed mixture. Add the dry ingredients and extracts. Drop by teaspoon (any size you want – just be consistent!) on the cookie sheets and bake for about 10 minutes. They should be nicely browned. Remove to brown paper. When slightly cooled, put a dab of the following icing on each.

Icing
1 cup **granulated sugar**
¼ cup **heavy cream**
1 teaspoon **vanilla extract**

Blend the sugar and the cream. Boil gently until a soft ball forms when dropped into cold water. Add vanilla and beat well.

MELISSA'S BISCOTTI
Yield: about 28 biscotti

These are GOOD! Melissa often mailed them to us from Virginia!

1 cup **granulated sugar**
1 ½ teaspoons **vanilla**
3 **eggs**, beaten
3 cups **all-purpose flour**
½ cup **chopped nuts or mini-chocolate morsels**
¾ teaspoon **baking soda**
¼ teaspoon **salt**

Preheat oven to 350 degrees and lightly grease cookie sheets. Beat together the sugar, vanilla and eggs. Combine flour, nuts or morsels, soda and salt; gradually add to sugar mixture beating to blend. Turn dough out onto floured board and knead 7 times. Shape into a 16 inch roll, place on baking sheet and flatten to 1 inch thick. Bake 30 minutes. With a serrated knife, slice the roll diagonally into thin slices. Reduce oven to 325 degrees and bake slices 10 minutes on one side. Turn slices and bake another 10 minutes. Cool on rack.

NOTE: This recipe allows for any number of variations in accordance with your epicurean peculiarities. Try dried cranberries and white chocolate!

NUT TAFFIES

Yield: 12 large or 24 small tarts

This is a Springfield recipe. They are rich and delicious. We made them often for Christmas and for tea parties!

¼ pound **butter** (1 stick)
1 cup sifted **flour**
3 ounces Philadelphia **cream cheese**
2 **eggs**
1 ½ cups **brown sugar**, firmly packed
2 tablespoons **melted butter**
½ teaspoon **vanilla**
½ teaspoon **salt**
1 cup **chopped pecans**

Preheat oven to 350 degrees. Mix first 3 ingredients with fingers, as you would with pie crust. Press in large or small ungreased muffin tins to form shells. Combine the next 6 ingredients for filling, reserving 1/8 cup nuts for topping. Fill each shell and sprinkle with reserved nuts. Bake for 15 minutes and 250 degrees for 10 minutes. Top with whipped cream, if you care to gild the lily!

OUR FAVORITE CHOCOLATE CHIP COOKIES
Yield: 4 dozen

A SUPER-SENSATIONAL cookie! Jeannie used to make this cookie often – giving most of them away to friends and neighbors.

1 cup **butter**
1 cup **brown sugar**, firmly packed
1 cup **white sugar**
2 teaspoons **vanilla extract**
2 tablespoons **milk**
2 **eggs**, lightly beaten
2 cups all-purpose flour
1 teaspoon **salt**
1 teaspoon **baking soda**
1 teaspoon **baking powder**
2 ½ cups **old-fashioned oats**
12 ounces **semi-sweet chocolate chips**
1 ½ cups **chopped walnuts**

Preheat the oven to 350 degrees. Cream the butter with the sugars in a mixer. Add the vanilla, milk and eggs. Add the flour, salt, baking soda and baking powder to the creamed mixture and beat to combine. By hand stir in the oats, chips and nuts. Drop 1 ½ inches apart on a greased cookie sheet. Bake for 10 to 12 minutes. Let sit 1 minute, then remove to cooling racks.

NOTE: Substitute raisins for the chocolate chips. That was always my favorite!

OATMEAL COOKIES
Yield: 5 dozen

These are very good cookies and easy to make. The only nuisance is to grind the raisins! It was fun to have a batch of warm cookies when you came home from school – just across the road in Solebury!

1 cup firmly packed **brown sugar**
1 cup granulated **sugar**
1 cup **butter or margarine**, room temperature
2 **eggs**
1 teaspoon **salt**
1 teaspoon **baking soda**
¼ cup **sour or sweet milk** (even water) to dissolve the soda
3 cups **quick oatmeal**
1 ½ cups **all-purpose flour**
1 cup **ground raisins**

Preheat oven to 375 and lightly grease cookie sheets. Cream the sugar and the butter thoroughly. Add the eggs and mix well. Add the milk with soda, oatmeal and flour. Again mix well. Add the raisins, distributing as evenly as possible. Drop by teaspoons on cookie sheet. Bake for about 10 minutes – until beautifully brown. You may want to bake half time on the lower rack and half time on upper rack.

Note: Leave a little space between cookies – they spread.

RUSSIAN TEA CAKES
Yield: 3 dozen

One of your mother's favorite Christmas cookies.

1 cup **butter** (it really must be butter!!)
½ cup **confectioners' sugar** with additional for rolling
1 teaspoon **vanilla**
2 ¼ cups sifted **all-purpose flour**
1 cup **pecans,** chopped

Preheat oven to 325 degrees and lightly spray cookie sheets. Cream butter and sugar thoroughly. Stir in vanilla, flour and pecans. Form into 1 inch balls and bake until lightly brown, 25 to 30 minutes. Roll in confectioners' sugar while hot. Allow to cool on brown paper and roll again in the confectioners' sugar.

TRINITY CHRISTMAS COOKIES
Yield: Approximately 250 cookies per recipe

One of the many happy memories of Solebury was the annual cookie bake for the Bazaar. It was a beautifully orchestrated project and the result of our labor was phenomenal. I will never forget one Sunday morning; the day after the last cookie had been packed away. At Coffee hour I noticed a young lady, obviously a visitor, so I walked over to welcome her. In the course of our conversation, I said, "Well, yesterday we finished our cookies. We rolled and baked and decorated 27,584 Christmas cookies." Her eyes widened, her mouth opened and she said, incredulously, "You count them?" Yes, indeed, we counted them!

Light Dough
1 pound **butter**
4 cups **granulated sugar**
1 cup **eggs** (4-5), well-beaten
¼ cup **water**
2 teaspoons **vanilla**
5 cups **all-purpose flour**
2 teaspoons **baking powder**

In a large bowl, cream butter and sugar. Add eggs, water and vanilla and mix well. Blend in flour and baking powder. Put dough in a plastic bowl and refrigerate over night.

Dark Dough
1 pound **butter**
2 cups **granulated sugar**
2 cups **light brown sugar**
1 cup **eggs** (4-5), well-beaten
6 teaspoons **baking powder**
2 teaspoons **nutmeg**
2 teaspoons **cinnamon**
2 teaspoons **cloves**
5 cups **all-purpose flour**
2 cups finely **ground walnuts**

In a large bowl, cream butter and sugars. Add eggs and mix well. Combine dry ingredients and add to the above. Put dough in a plastic bag and refrigerate overnight.

The Next Day…

When ready to bake, preheat oven to 325 degrees and grease cookie sheets. Using a small amount of dough each time, roll out to 1/8 inch thickness on well-floured pastry cloth, and cut into festive shapes. Bake for 8-10 minutes or until lightly browned. Remove from cookie sheets immediately.

Decorating Hints: Before baking, cookies can be brushed with egg white mixed with a little water and food coloring. After baking, cookies can be frosted with a mixture of confectioners' sugar, then sprinkled with colored sugar or non-pareils.

Note: Do not use food coloring in the egg whites with the dark dough.

SHORT BREAD FOR MOLDS
Yield: your choice

Shades of Christmas in Solebury. We made these by the hundreds for our annual bazaar. Many of the women had interesting butter molds which we used. Mrs. Sanford had one that measured 12 inches across. GORGEOUS!

1 pound **butter** (It must be butter!)
2 1/3 cups **confectioners' sugar**
1 **egg**
5 ½ cups **all-purpose flour**

Preheat oven to 300 degrees. Cream thoroughly the butter and sugar. Add the egg and mix well again. Add some flour. This much can be done in the electric mixer. Add the rest of the flour, a little at a time, stirring with a spoon. Knead with your hands until the right consistency. It should get a little waxy. Knead until the "bowl is clean." Put on waxed paper what you would consider enough dough for your mold. Flatten to about 1 inch and sprinkle with Wondra flour and press on mold. With sharp knife cut excess from around mold and smooth sides carefully with side of knife. Transfer to an ungreased cookie pan and bake about 30 minutes. Watch carefully. It should be a lovely light tan.

NOTE: Wondra is superfine flour with a dusty texture that doesn't clump. There is no substitute for Wondra!

CAKES

I REMEMBER . . . when I was growing up, all cakes were made from "scratch." When the "cake mix" came on the market, Mother gave them a try, but used them rarely. Although we used them more as the years went by, we always thought our special cakes were best. Except for the angel food. I must confess I have not made an angel food cake except from a box for many, many years.

And that was my favorite when I was growing up – that was what I requested for my birthday cake. I can still see Mother making it. She put 12 egg whites on a platter and with a hand whisk and wide strokes she transformed her raw material into a great white mountain. Powdered sugar icing, candles and some "decoration" made it into the pièce de résistance at my birthday parties.

 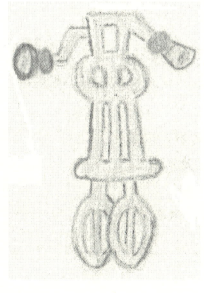

MAYO-RAISIN CAKE
Yield: One 9x13 cake

After eating a piece of this, Jeannie said, "This is the best cake I've ever eaten!"

3 cups sifted **all-purpose flour**
2 cups **granulated sugar**
1 cup **mayonnaise**
1/3 cup **milk**
2 **eggs**
2 teaspoons **baking soda**
1 ½ teaspoons **ground cinnamon**
½ teaspoon **ground nutmeg**
½ teaspoon **salt**
¼ teaspoon **ground cloves**
3 cups peeled and **chopped apples**
1 cup **seedless raisins**
½ cup **chopped nuts** (optional)

Preheat oven to 350 degrees. Grease and flour two 9 inch round baking pans or one 9x13 inch pan. With mixer at low speed, beat first 10 ingredients 2 minutes, scraping bowl frequently. Stir in apples, raisins and nuts and pour into pans. Bake 45 minutes or until cake tester inserted in center comes out clean. Cool in pans 10 minutes. Remove and cool.

NOTE: The round cakes are lovely filled and frosted with 2 cups whipped cream.

APPLE CAKE
Yield: One 9x9 cake

Ginny Saunders' recipe. This is a good and moist cake which can be served as is or with whipped cream or vanilla ice cream.

1 cup sifted **all-purpose flour**
1 cup **granulated sugar**
½ teaspoon **baking powder**
½ teaspoon **baking soda**
½ teaspoon **cinnamon**
½ teaspoon **salt**
1 **egg**, beaten
¼ pound (1 stick) **butter or margarine**, melted
1 cup **chopped nuts**
3 cups **peeled and chopped apples**

Preheat oven to 325 degrees and grease a 9x9 inch pan. Mix first 8 ingredients together. Add 1 cup nuts (optional) and 3 cups peeled and chopped apples. Put batter in pan and bake for about 45 minutes.

CARROT CAKE

Yield: One 8-inch layered cake

The ultimate compliment! After his first taste, John Root asked for the recipe. Unequivocally, this is the best carrot cake in the world!

4 **eggs**
1 ½ cups **oil**
2 cups **grated carrots**
2 cups **granulated sugar**
2 cups sifted **all-purpose flour**
2 teaspoons **cinnamon**
1 ½ teaspoons **salt**
1 ½ teaspoons **baking soda**

Preheat the oven to 350 degrees and grease and flour three round 8 inch cake pans. Combine eggs, oil and carrots and beat well. Combine dry ingredients and add to the first mixture. Beat. Put in pans and bake for about 30 minutes.

Pineapple icing:

1 – 8 ounce package Philadelphia **cream cheese**
¼ pound **butter** (1 stick)
1 – 1 pound box **confectioners' sugar**
2 teaspoons **vanilla**
1 small can **crushed pineapple**, well-drained
1 cup **nuts,** optional

Cream together thoroughly the cream cheese and the butter. Gradually beat in the confectioners' sugar. Add the vanilla, the pineapple and the nuts.

To Assemble: Frost and stack. Perhaps a toothpick or two will help to hold the layers together.

CLARICE'S CHOCOLATE CAKE
Yield: One 13x9 cake or one 8 inch layered cake

Making a cake from "scratch" is a very satisfying experience – in more ways than one! Clarice Johnson was a friend of mine way back in my teaching days in Elbow Lake, MN.

1 ½ cups **granulated sugar**
½ cup **butter** (1 stick)
2 **eggs**, well-beaten
2 squares **unsweetened chocolate**, melted
2 cups sifted **cake flour**
½ cup **milk**
½ cup **water**
1 teaspoon **baking soda** dissolved in 2 teaspoons cold water

Preheat oven to 350 degrees and grease and flour two round cake pans or one 13x9 pan. Cream sugar and butter. Add the eggs and then the chocolate. Add flour and liquids, alternately, always beginning and ending with flour. Add soda last. Bake for about 35 minutes. Test for doneness!

NOTE: When creaming butter and sugar in any recipe, beat a long time – until it is no longer grainy.

DELICIOUS CAKE
Yield: One bundt cake

When recipes such as this one came out in the early '60s, we thought they were ambrosia. Now after all these years we continue to consider them excellent – moist with good texture and good taste.

1 package **lemon cake mix** (without butter)
1 cup **water**
1 package **instant lemon pudding**
4 **eggs**
½ cup **oil**

Preheat oven to 350 degrees and grease and flour a bundt pan. Beat all ingredients together for 3 minutes. Put batter in pan and bake 1 hour. After it has been out of the oven for 15 minutes, glaze with the following mixture: 1/3 cup lemon juice 1/3 cup granulated sugar. When cool, remove from pan.

FEATHER CAKE
Yield: One 9x13 cake

One of Grandma Everson's favorites! This is delicious when served with strawberries or fresh peaches and whipped cream. Real whipped cream!

- 2 cups **all-purpose flour**
- 2 teaspoons **baking powder**
- 5 **eggs**
- 2 cups **granulated sugar**
- 1 cup **boiling water**

Preheat oven to 350 degree. Sift the flour together with the baking powder several times. Separate eggs. Beat the yolks and sugar a long time – at least 15 minutes – until it is thick and lemon colored and satin smooth. Beat the egg whites until they form stiff peaks. Fold the egg whites into the yolks, and then the flour into the egg mixture. Stir in the boiling water. Bake in an ungreased 9x13 inch pan for about 45 minutes. Invert pan to cool.

NOTE: A good way to test for doneness with a sponge cake such as this is to touch it lightly with your finger. If it springs back and if the sizzling has stopped, it is done.

HOT MILK CUSTARD CHIFFON CAKE
Yield: One cake

I remember the first time I made this. I felt like I had discovered a gold mine!

2 cups sifted **all-purpose flour**
1 cup cooking **oil**
1½ cups fine **granulated sugar**
2 teaspoons **vanilla**
3 teaspoons **baking powder**
8 **egg yolks**, beaten very thick
1 teaspoon **salt**
8 **egg whites**, stiffly beaten
¾ cup scalding **hot milk**
1 teaspoon **cream of tartar**

Preheat oven to 325 degrees. Sift flour, sugar, baking powder and salt into large bowl. Add scalding hot milk and beat to mix well. Then add oil, vanilla and thoroughly beaten egg yolks. Mix well. Beat egg whites until foamy throughout; sprinkle with cream of tartar and beat until very stiff. Pour the egg yolk mixture over the beaten egg whites gradually, gently folding them together with a rubber scraper until blended. Pour batter into an ungreased ten-inch tube pan and bake about 55 minutes. Turn pan upside down to let air circulate under it while cake cools. Remove from pan.

NOTE: You may want a light icing, but it is certainly not necessary.

JEWISH APPLE CAKE
Yield: One cake

This was one of Grandma Everson's favorite cakes – with good reason. It's delicious!

½ cup **granulated sugar**
2 teaspoons **cinnamon**
4 **eggs**
2 cups **granulated sugar**
1 cup **oil**
3 cups sifted **all-purpose flour**
3 teaspoons **baking powder**
½ teaspoon **salt**
½ cup **orange or pineapple juice**
2 ½ teaspoons **vanilla**
3 cups **peeled and sliced apples** (4 medium sized apples)
confectioners' sugar

Preheat oven to 350 degrees and grease and flour a 10 inch tube pan. In small bowl, mix ½ cup sugar and 2 teaspoons cinnamon. In large bowl, beat eggs and gradually beat in the 2 cups sugar. Add the oil and mix well. Sift the flour with the baking powder and the salt. Add the flour to the egg mixture in small amounts, alternately with small amounts of juice. Beat in vanilla. Pour ¼ of the batter into the pan. On this batter put 1/3 of the apple slices and 1/3 of the cinnamon mixture. Repeat in this order until all the ingredients are used, ending with a layer of batter. Bake 1 hour, or until toothpick comes out clean. Cool ½ hour and remove from pan. Sprinkle with confectioner's sugar if desired.

MOTHER'S ORANGE DATE CAKE
Yield: One 9x13 cake

Grandma Everson used to make this a lot. It's a substantial cake with good flavor.

1 cup **granulated sugar**
½ cup **butter or margarine**
2 **eggs**
1 teaspoon **baking soda**
1 cup **buttermilk**
2 cups **all-purpose sifted flour**
1 teaspoon **baking powder**
1 teaspoon **salt**
1 tablespoon **grated orange rind**
½ cup **chopped nuts**
1 cup **dates**, cut in quarters

Preheat oven to 325 degrees and grease and flour a 9x13 pan. Cream the butter and sugar. Add the eggs one at a time, beating well after each addition. Stir soda into buttermilk and add alternately with the flour, baking powder and salt, beginning and ending with flour. Add rind, nuts and dates and mix gently.

Syrup:

¾ cup **granulated sugar**
½ cup **orange juice**
1 tablespoon **grated orange rind**

Combine in a saucepan. Slowly bring to a boil and immediately remove from heat. Bake the cake for about 45 minutes, until a cake tester comes out dry. Remove from oven and pour the syrup over the top of the cake. Allow the cake to stand in the pan until completely cold and all the syrup has been absorbed.

1-2-3-4 CAKE

Yield: One cake

This was Maggie Root's favorite cake!

1 cup **butter**
2 cups **confectioners' sugar**
4 **eggs**, beaten
1 teaspoon **vanilla**
2 teaspoons **baking powder**
1 teaspoon **salt**
3 cups sifted **all-purpose flour**
1 cup warm **milk**

Preheat oven to 350 degrees. Grease and flour a tube pan or three 8 inch round cake pans. Cream sugar and butter for 15 minutes. Add eggs and vanilla. Add baking powder to the flour and mix well into the batter, alternating with the milk, and beginning and ending with flour. Pour into pans. Bake for 1 hour. Always test for doneness.

EASY CHOCOLATE FROSTING

You always loved those little marshmallows.

2 – one ounce squares **unsweetened chocolate**
2 cups **tiny marshmallows**
¼ cup **water**
¼ cup **butter**
2 cups **confectioners' sugar**
1 teaspoon **vanilla**
½ cup **chopped nuts** (optional)

In a saucepan melt and heat together the chocolate, 1 cup marshmallows, water and butter. Cool slightly. Add the confectioners' sugar and vanilla and beat for 2 minutes. Fold in the remaining marshmallows.

FLUFFY WHITE FROSTING

I used to make this a lot. Sometimes it is called "Mock Whipped Cream Frosting" – pretty good name!

½ cup **milk**
2 ½ tablespoons **flour**
½ cup **butter**
½ cup **granulated sugar**
1 teaspoon **vanilla**

Mix the milk and flour in a covered jar. Shake until well mixed. Cook until a paste, stirring constantly. Cool. Cream butter, sugar and vanilla. Beat until fluffy at medium speed of mixer. Add paste and beat at high speed, until creamy.

NOTE: In my mother's kitchen we had a device called a flour shaker for mixing ingredients as in the first step of this recipe. I haven't seen one for years, but a covered jar will do.

HARVEST MOON FROSTING

As you might guess, this recipe never fails! From my friend Lillie Magnuson in Bemidji.

4 tablespoons **butter**
4 tablespoons **cream**
6 tablespoons **brown sugar**
2 cups **confectioners' sugar**
1 teaspoon **vanilla**

In a saucepan bring the butter, cream and brown sugar to a boil. Add the confectioners' sugar and vanilla and beat well.

NEVER FAIL FROSTING

We used to call this "7 Minute Frosting" – that's about right. This is especially nice on a white, yellow or chocolate cake.

2 **egg whites**
6 tablespoons **water**
3 tablespoons **corn syrup**
½ teaspoon **baking powder**
1 cup **granulated sugar** or 1 ¼ cups firmly packed **brown sugar**
1 teaspoon **vanilla**

Put all the ingredients, except the vanilla, in the top of a double boiler. Beat with an electric beater, over boiling water, until it forms thick peaks. Remove from fire and fill the bottom half of the double boiler with cold water. Add vanilla and continue to beat until it is very thick.

BEVERAGES

I REMEMBER . . . friends who came to our home, expected or unexpected, were not there very long before they were offered some liquid refreshment. Mother told me that when I was little, and when someone came to call, I would very soon whisper in her ear, "May I make coffee?," a truly Norwegian tradition I'm sure. Today we tend to offer iced drinks. "Real" coffee is reserved for breakfast and "decaf" for after dinner!

ICED TEA PUNCH

Yield: 12 – 6 ounce servings

This was served often at St. Martin's, Radnor. The recipe came from the files of Alison Henderson.

6 **tea bags** steeped in 1 **pint water**
1 – 12 ounce can **lemonade concentrate**
1 – 12 ounce can **orange juice concentrate**
1 quart **soda water**
1 quart **orange ice** (not sherbet)

Put tea, lemonade and orange juice in punch bowl. When ready to serve, pour in soda and place a quart orange ice (not sherbet) in bowl. Garnish with sliced oranges, lemons and strawberries.

LEMON BEER PUNCH
Yield: 6 – 6 ounce servings

This is a Puerto Rican recipe from my friend Tecla Sund Reklau.

1 cup **sugar**
1 cup **water**
all the **lemon rinds**
1 cup **lemon juice**
½ cup **grapefruit juice**
1 – 12 ounce – **bottle light beer**
fresh lemon slices
whole cloves

Mix sugar and water in a heavy pot and bring to the boiling point. Add rinds, cover and let stand 5 minutes. Remove rinds and cool syrup. Add fruit juices and pour into a punch bowl over ice. Add beer just before serving. Float lemon slices studded with cloves on punch.

LEMON SANGRIA

Yield: 10 - 4 ounce glasses

Very refreshing!

3 ½ cups **dry white wine**, chilled
3 unpeeled **lemons**, sliced
1 unpeeled **orange**, sliced
small bunches **green grapes**
½ cup **Cognac**
¼ cup **sugar**
1 – 10 ounce – bottle **club soda**, chilled
ice cubes

Combine all ingredients except soda and ice cubes in large pitcher and chill overnight. Just before serving, add soda and ice cubes and stir lightly. Pour into glasses, adding fruit as desired.

RHINE VALLEY PUNCH
Yield: 15 small cups

We served this first at Dad's Institution at Holy Trinity and the Celebration of his 50th Birthday. It was quite a hit!

¼ cup **peach brandy**
¼ cup **Benedictine**
2 **oranges**, sliced thin
1 **lemon**, sliced thin
2 sprigs **fresh mint**
2 Fifths **Rhine wine**, iced
1 cup hulled **strawberries**
Block of **ice**

Combine peach brandy, Benedictine, sliced fruit and mint in bowl. Mix, cover and let stand for 2 hours. Place block of ice in chilled punch bowl. Pour peach brandy mixture over ice and add strawberries. Pour wine in and stir gently.

CANDY

I REMEMBER . . . as children we often made candy – chocolate fudge, penuche or divinity. The result was not always successful. It was sometimes too hard or sometimes too soft, but we didn't seem to care. It was never wasted!

BAKED CARAMEL CORN
Yield: about 6 quarts

This is addictive!

1 cup (2 sticks) **butter**
2 cups firmly packed **brown sugar**
½ cup **white corn syrup**
1 teaspoon **salt**
½ teaspoon **baking soda**
1 teaspoon **vanilla**
6 quarts **popcorn**

Melt butter in two quart saucepan. Stir in sugar, corn syrup and salt. Bring to a boil, stirring constantly. Boil, without stirring, 5 minutes. Remove from heat; stir in soda and vanilla. Gradually pour over popped corn, mixing well. Turn into two large shallow baking pans with rims. Bake in a preheated 250 degree oven 1 hour, stirring every fifteen minutes. Remove from oven and cool completely. Break apart in large chunks and store in tightly covered containers.

NOTE: A lovely addition would be some nuts – pecans, almonds, peanuts – whatever suits your fancy. If you do add nuts, spread them on a shallow pan and roast in a preheated 350 degree oven for about 10 minutes. Stir the nuts into the syrup and then pour it over the warmed popcorn, stirring with a wooden spoon.

BUTTER CREAM EASTER EGGS
Yield: Enough

Another Solebury recipe – from Tess Sands. We had fun making these and eating them! Many times we put decorations on them, a tiny leaf and flower, using a cake decorator.

¼ pound **butter,** softened
1 – 8 ounce package of Philadelphia **cream cheese**
2 – 1 pound boxes of **confectioners' sugar**
1 teaspoon **vanilla**

Mix butter and cream cheese together and beat well. Add 2 – 1 pound boxes of confectioners' sugar and 1 teaspoon vanilla. Using about 2 tablespoons of the mixture, shape into eggs. Place on wax paper on cookie sheets and refrigerate overnight.

1 – 8 ounce box of Baker's **semi-sweet chocolate**
½ slab of **wax** (2 ounces)

In the morning put in top of double boiler chocolate and ½ slab of wax. Melt together. Spoon chilled eggs into hot chocolate and place on wax paper. Refrigerate. When chocolate hardens, decorate or maybe not. Your choice.

NOTE: Wax usually comes in a one pound carton with four slabs, each 4 ounces.

JIMMY CARTER'S FAVORITE PEANUT BRITTLE

Yield: 2 pounds

If this recipe is good enough for Jimmy, it should be good enough for us! It is wonderful!

3 cups **granulated sugar**
1 ½ cups **water**
1 cup **white corn syrup**
3 cups **raw peanuts**
½ stick (4 ounces) **butter**
2 tablespoons **baking soda**
1 teaspoon **vanilla**

Boil sugar, water and syrup without stirring, until it spins a thread. This will take about 30 minutes on medium heat. Add peanuts and butter and stir continuously until syrup turns golden brown, about 20 minutes. Remove from heat and add the soda and the vanilla. Pour on two cookie sheets with rims. As mixture begins to harden around edges, pull until thin. Cool completely. Break into pieces and store in tightly covered containers.

POPCORN BALLS

Yield: 12 large balls

This recipe is from Jeannie's friend, Holly Nichols, from Solebury. Many a Sunday afternoon we had this treat made by the little girls!

1 cup **molasses**
1 cup **granulated sugar**
1 tablespoon **vinegar**
2 tablespoons **butter**
½ teaspoon **baking soda**
12 cups **popcorn**, popped that is!

Combine first 4 ingredients. Cook over medium heat, stirring occasionally until a small amount forms a hard ball in cold water. Remove from heat and add soda. Pour over corn and gently mix. Butter fingers and mold into balls.

VANILLA CARAMELS
Yield: 2 pounds

This is a Springfield recipe. And Jean is the expert! She has never had a failure. And the caramels – they are divine!

- 2 cups **granulated sugar**
- 2 cups **warm light cream**
- 1 cup **white corn syrup**
- ½ teaspoon **salt**
- 1/3 cup **butter**
- 1 teaspoon **vanilla**
- 1 cup **chopped nuts** (optional)

Mix sugar, 1 cup of the cream, corn syrup and salt in a large heavy saucepan. Boil gently, stirring constantly, for about 10 minutes. Add remaining cream slowly. Boil 5 minutes longer. Stir in butter, a little at a time. Boil slowly, stirring, until a small amount of mixture forms a firm ball when dropped into cold water. Remove from heat; add vanilla and nuts. Mix. Pour into buttered pan 9x9x2 inches and cool. Cut into squares and wrap each in waxed paper. Refrigerate.

SWEET AND SOUR

I REMEMBER ... Mother had a room in our basement where she stored her canned goods. It was lined with shelves and was very cool. In the fall there were literally hundreds of mason jars filled with peaches, pears, apricots and kosher dill pickles. She rarely canned vegetables; Mr. Stokely did that for us. Besides all this there was always a 100 pound bag of Red River Valley potatoes which my Uncle Murray sent to us every fall and my Dad's Cuban cigars!

The canning that I did as you were growing up was minimal to be sure. I did make special jams, jellies, chutneys, relishes and pickles but not in any large quantity. It was fun to use the bounty of the harvest in new and interesting recipes.

CRANBERRY RELISH

Another family favorite – I give my Mother credit for this recipe.

2 cups **cranberries**
1 large **seedless orange**, rind and all
2 cups **granulated sugar**

Put cranberries and orange through the food grinder. Add sugar and let "ripen" two or three days in the refrigerator.

NOTE: This will keep indefinitely in the refrigerator.

FRUIT JAM

I wonder if we will ever preserve fruits and vegetables as my Mother did. Just in case, this recipe is from my Aunt Hilda, Grandma's sister. This is an easy and good recipe and can be used with almost any fruit. I used this after Mason Brower and I had been on our hands and knees for several hours picking wild strawberries!

4 cups **boiling water**
4 cups of **fruit**
3 cups of **granulated sugar**

Pour 4 cups boiling water over 4 cups of fruit. Drain immediately. Add 2 cups of granulated sugar to the fruit. Mix well and boil 3 minutes. Add 1 more cup of sugar and boil 5 minutes. Let stand until the next morning, stirring once in a while. Wash and sterilize jars. Reheat jam and fill jars. If you don't have tight lids, pour a thin layer of melted parafin wax on the top.

Note: To sterilize jars, put them upside down together with the covers in about 3 inches of boiling water, and boil gently for about 5 minutes.

RHUBARB MARMALADE

This is so easy to make and the taste is superior to almost any commercial product!

1 **lemon**
1 **orange**
1 ¾ pounds **rhubarb,** cut into small pieces
1/3 cup **golden raisins**
3 ¼ cups **granulated sugar**

Squeeze the lemon and orange and reserve the juice. Remove white pulp and finely chop the rinds. Combine with rhubarb, raisins, sugar and let it sit overnight. Add the juice of the lemon and orange to the rhubarb and cook until thick, stirring frequently. Put in sterilized jelly jars while hot and seal with canning lids or hot paraffin.

SPICY CRANBERRY CONSERVE

A great combination of ingredients. Keeps for at least a month in the refrigerator.

1 – 12 ounce jar **orange marmalade**
2 cups **fresh cranberries**, rinsed and picked over
½ teaspoon ground **allspice**
½ teaspoon **ground cloves**
3 inch **cinnamon stick**
1 – 16 ounce can or jar **small whole onions**, drained
1 – 8 ounce can **chunky pineapple**, drained
1 cup toasted **coarsely chopped walnuts**

Combine the marmalade, cranberries, allspice, cloves and cinnamon in a medium-size saucepan. Cook over medium-high heat, stirring frequently, until the cranberries begin to pop, about 5 to 10 minutes. Stir in the onions, pineapple, and walnuts and cook for 3 minutes longer, stirring constantly. Remove from the heat and let cool slightly. Turn into a bowl or container with a tight-fitting lid and refrigerate until serving time. Serve chilled, at room temperature or slightly warm.

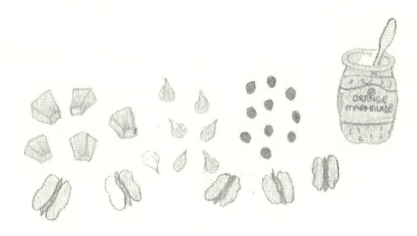

ZUCCHINI PICKLES
Yield: 3 pints

This wonderful recipe is from our dear friend, Anne Surgent. She supplied us with jars of these delicious pickles for all our holidays and special events.

2 pounds small **zucchini**
2 medium sized **onions**
¼ cup **salt**
2 cups **white vinegar**
2 cups **granulated sugar**
1 teaspoon **celery seed**
1 teaspoon **turmeric**
2 teaspoons **mustard seed**

Wash zucchini and cut them in very thin slices. Peel and quarter the onions and cut into thin slices. Cover the vegetables with ice water. Add salt and let stand 2 hours. Drain thoroughly. Bring remaining ingredients to a boil and pour over vegetables. Let stand 2 hours. Bring the vegetables and syrup to a boil and boil for 5 minutes. Pack in hot sterilized jars and seal.

THE SMÖRGASBORD

Breaking bread together, sharing food, "sleeping over" are not modern phenomena. That's been going on for centuries—way back in the days of the Vikings.

You see, in the days of the Vikings the distances were long and family and friends rarely got together. When they did they brought food and stayed for days and weeks. The smörgasbord became a central part of these reunions. A simple definition of smörgasbord is a buffet meal of various hot and cold food. Smörgas (sandwich) and bord (table).

The Scandinavians brought this tradition to their new home in America centuries later and to this day the smörgasbord is an important part of their celebrations. Today it is still a table laden with a great variety of good eating; but, I think, for the most part, the guests go home before bedtime!

In our home and pretty much the Norwegian community in which I was raised, we celebrated the holidays with Scandinavian delicacies but not in the pattern of the soup to nuts Smörgasbords that we read about.

I REMEMBER . . . before Christmas, Mother baked Lefse, Yulekage and a dozen or so varieties of cookies. During the holiday season when anyone "came to call," they were brought out, placed on pretty trays and enjoyed with good strong coffee. After the guests left, they all were packed away in tins until the next friend knocked on the door.

Growing up, Jeannie always had a great interest in her Scandinavian heritage and the ways we celebrated the traditions in our own family. She always thought it would be fun to have a "real" Smörgasbord. So one year while living in Philadelphia, she planned and orchestrated a beautiful Norwegian feast for the Vestry of the Church of the Holy Trinity.

On her long table draped with white damask, she constructed two tiers which she covered with white cloth and live greenery. This allowed her more space to display the various dishes. Because her space was limited, she provided 3 different settings:
   —a perfect table of appetizers
   —the main course
   —a sweet finale

It seems that the appetizer course is the most popular in Scandinavian dining—most lavish and abundant, with sometimes 30 – 50 different foods appearing. Needless to say, Jeannie had to limit her offerings. But she did have pickled herring, smoked salmon, liver paté, pickled beets, several kinds of cheese (gjetost and Gouda among them), and deviled eggs with sardines and anchovies. She served lefse, knackerbröd (crisp rye bread) and limpa (soft sweet light rye with molasses).

For the second setting she featured meatballs, baked ham and creamed finnan haddie, a good substitute she thought for lutefisk! She rounded out this course with baked brown beans, cabbage salad with the traditional whipped cream and vinegar dressing, celery and apple salad and marinated cucumbers. The finnan haddie was especially good – we used a new recipe learned from our fish man. He said, "Reduce to half one quart of light cream. Add the fish and heat thoroughly."

On to the third and last course – she offered a full array of traditional sweets:

—Sandbakkels filled with lingonberries and topped with whipped cream
—Berline Kranser
—Fattimand
—Krum Kake
—Rosettes

Glögg, the traditional Christmas beverage, was served, followed by cold beer and good strong coffee. It was a memorable evening!

NOTE: Dad and Jean and I found out on our trip to Scandinavia in the summer of 2000 that the Smörgasbord is still alive and well! We were overwhelmed by the tables heavy with food, and those tables throughout Norway, Sweden, Denmark and Finland held the same delicacies for breakfast, lunch and dinner. Can you believe seven varieties of herring for breakfast? We quickly adapted!

BERLINER KRANSER
Yield: 4 dozen

There are many recipes with minor variations for this delicious and delicate Norwegian cookie. But after years of baking this cookie, Mother and I decided on this one. Mother always said the hard boiled yolks made the difference!

3 **hard boiled egg yolks**
4 **raw egg yolks**
1 cup **granulated sugar**
4 cups sifted **all-purpose flour**
1 pound **unsalted butter** (no substitutions)
4 **egg whites**
coarse white sugar

Preheat oven to 350 degrees and grease cookie sheets. Mash thoroughly the hard boiled yolks. Beat the raw egg yolks with the granulated sugar until they are thick and lemon colored. Mix the flour and the butter as for pie crust. Now mix all the ingredients together, except the egg whites. Beat the egg whites until frothy. Take a small amount of dough and roll it with your hands into a rope. Form it into a wreath. Dip the wreaths completely into the egg whites and then dip one side into the coarse white sugar and place on the cookie sheets. At this time you may put slivers of candied green cherries and a piece of red cherry at the point where the dough is crossed to form the wreath. Bake about 15 minutes until delicately brown.

CABBAGE SALAD

Yield: 6-8 servings

No mayonnaise! The whipped cream makes it a lighter, fresher salad.

1/2 head of **cabbage**
2 tablespoons **granulated sugar**
3 or more tablespoons **vinegar**
1/2 pint **heavy cream**

Cut up cabbage, fine. Mix in sugar, vinegar, salt and pepper to taste. Whip cream stiff and mix with cabbage.

NOTE: This should not be made too far in advance of your serving.

CELERY APPLE SALAD
Yield: 6 servings

3/4 cup **walnut halves**
3 large **apples**
1 1/2 tablespoons freshly squeezed **lemon juice**
2 stalks **celery**, sliced on the diagonal
1/2 cup **mayonnaise**
2 tablespoons **sour cream**
3/4 teaspoon **lemon zest**
1 teaspoon **sugar**

Spread the nuts on a baking sheet and toast for 8 to 10 minutes. Cut the apples into 3/4 inch pieces. In a bowl mix the apples with the lemon juice, celery and walnuts. In a bowl whisk together the mayonnaise, sour cream, lemon zest and sugar. Add the dressing to the apple mixture and stir to coat. Refrigerate until ready to serve.

DANISH KRINGLE

Yield: 4 large bars

I can't count the times we have made this delicacy through the years. An exceptionally good recipe.

Dough

4 cups **all-purpose flour**
1 cup **butter or margarine** (butter is better)
1 cup **milk**, scalded and cooled
3 beaten **egg yolks**
1 package **dry yeast**
3 tablespoons **sugar**

Filling

1 cup **softened butter** (1/4 cup on each bar)
3 **egg whites**, beaten
2 cups **brown sugar** (1/2 cup on each bar)
chopped nuts

Confectioners' Sugar Glaze

2 cups **confectioners' sugar**
Enough **milk**, about 2 tablespoons, for drizzling consistency.

Mix the first 2 ingredients as you would a piecrust. Mix the next 4 ingredients in a separate bowl and pour over the flour and butter mixture to make soft dough. Chill over night or two hours in the freezer. Divide the dough into 4 parts. Roll each one into a rectangle, the thinner the better. Spread each one with a layer of softened butter, beaten egg white, and brown sugar. Fold 1 side over 1/3. Lay the other side over on top (3 layers). Let rise 2 hours. When ready to bake, preheat the oven to 350 degrees. Bake for about 20 minutes. Frost immediately with confectioners' sugar glaze. Sprinkle with chopped nuts if desired.

Note: When I make this, I usually bake the Kringle 10 minutes on each shelf. This allows it to brown evenly on the top and on the bottom. I usually sprinkle chopped walnuts on top of the glaze, except if John is going to indulge. When the Kringle is for John, no nuts.

DELICIOUS BAKED BEANS
Yield: Lots

A professor's wife from Bemidji State College, Mrs. Ray Carlson, gave me this recipe. Now you can't find a better recipe for baked beans than this. Today we tend to jazz up a can or two of baked beans and they're tasty. But just try these! Wonderful addition to a picnic table or Smörgasbörd!

2 pounds small **navy beans**
1 **onion**, chopped
½ pound **browned bacon** square, cut in small pieces
molasses, a few dollops
brown sugar, a tablespoon or two
catsup or tomato sauce, a bottle or so – you be the judge
salt, a little

Soak the beans in water overnight or use the quick soak method. Drain. Combine all ingredients and cover with water. Preheat oven to 325 degrees. Put in a greased casserole with a good cover and bake for several hours. Check from time to time – stir and add more water if necessary.

NOTE: "Quick soak method" can be found on most packages of dried legumes.

FATTIMAND

Yield: about 6 dozen

These "fried" cookies are delicious! Many nationalities have a variation on this theme, but, of course, the Norwegians have them all beat!

6 **egg yolks**
1/3 cup **granulated sugar**
1/8 teaspoon **cinnamon**
½ teaspoon **crushed cardamom seed** (or more!)
¼ teaspoon **grated lemon rind**
1 tablespoon **brandy**
1/3 cup **cream**, whipped
3 **egg whites**, stiffly beaten
2 ½ cups sifted **all-purpose flour**

Beat egg yolks until they are thick and lemon colored. Combine sugar, cinnamon, cardamom and gradually add to egg yolks, beating until very light. Add lemon rind and brandy. Fold in cream and egg whites. Gradually stir in flour until dough is stiff enough to handle. Chill. Take a portion of the dough and roll out as thin as possible. Cut into rectangles about 4 inches x 2 inches (or smaller if you like). Make a small slash in the center of the rectangle. Take one corner of the rectangle and pull it carefully through the slash. Fry in hot grease. After a few seconds in the grease, turn. When light brown, remove and place on paper towels. They fry quickly! The paper towels will absorb the excess grease.

NOTE: Grandma Everson had a special little pastry cutter – a small serrated circle which rotated. It was, of course, attached to a wooden handle. It made a decorative edge on the fattimand. Check the doughnut recipe for a test to determine the proper oil temperature for frying.

GLÖGG

Yield: 15 – 3 ounce servings

This recipe came from Aunt Viv. We used to serve this at our annual vestry party which was held in December. With it we served all our Scandinavian delicacies. Do you remember?

1 ounce **bitters** (angostura)
¾ cup **granulated sugar**
1 pint **claret**
1 pint **sherry**
½ pint **brandy**

Put all the above ingredients into a large casserole and heat until piping hot.

To serve: Put one golden raisin and one unsalted almond in an old-fashion glass and fill it ¾ full. (A spoon in the glass before pouring in the hot liquid prevents the glass from cracking.) Actually, if you recall, I served this in our beautiful china teacups.

KJÖTTBALLAR

Yield: 6 servings

Translated: Very good meatballs!

½ cup **milk**
2 **eggs**
½ cup **soft bread crumbs**
¾ pound **ground beef**
¼ pound **lean ground pork**
¼ pound **ground veal**
1 teaspoon **ground nutmeg**
¾ teaspoon **ground ginger**
½ teaspoon ground **allspice**
2 teaspoons **salt**
¼ teaspoon **pepper**
2 tablespoons **minced onion**
butter

Preheat oven to 400 degrees. Beat milk and eggs together and pour over bread crumbs. When soft, mix with the meat which has been ground twice and work well together. Add spices and onions, sauteed until limp. Work all together until light and fluffy. Form in small balls and brown in butter in a heavy skillet and place on ungreased jelly roll pan, 15 ½ x 10 ½ x 1 inch and bake for about 20 minutes.

Note: Finely ground beef, veal and pork and the combination of spices make these meatballs typically Norwegian. Buy ground beef, pork and veal; then ask the butcher to grind it again.

KNACKERBRÖD

Yield: 3 - 4 large rounds

This is a good snack anytime - with or without butter!

1/2 cup **butter,** melted
1/4 cup **sugar**
1/2 cup **oatmeal flour**
1 cup **graham flour**
3/4 teaspoon **baking soda**
1 teaspoon **salt**
1 1/2 cups **buttermilk**
3 - 4 cups **all-purpose flour**

Preheat oven to 350 degrees. Combine ingredients, adding just enough white flour to make dough workable. Roll out into rounds using grooved rolling pin. Bake on a cookie sheet for about 8 minutes until crisp.

KRUMKAKE
Yield: 3 dozen

Another Norwegian treasure. There are many recipes that vary only slightly. This one is from Jane Brynjolfson Wallace, one of our dear friends since childhood.

4 **eggs**
1 cup **granulated sugar**
1 ½ cups **all-purpose flour**
¾ cup **melted butter**. And it must be butter!
½ teaspoon **salt**
1 teaspoon **vanilla**

Beat the 4 eggs until light and lemon colored. Add the sugar, flour, butter, salt and vanilla. Spoon one to two tablespoons of dough on a preheated krumkake iron. Close cover and bake until lightly brown. Remove from iron and roll into a cylinder.

NOTE: We have a very old krumkake iron that my mother always used. It is one that is put directly on the burner. Jane suggests an electric iron because it is easier to regulate.

LEFSE
Yield: about 2 dozen

This is Grandma Everson's recipe and it is a good one! The true Norwegian spread a lefse on a dinner plate, covered it with lutefisk (cod soaked in lye and boiled) and lots of drawn butter, rolled it up and enjoyed! In my home we mostly just spread it with butter and sprinkled it with sugar. But we always rolled it up to eat.

FOR EACH 3 CUPS OF RICED POTATOES:
5 tablespoons **shortening or lard**
1 tablespoon **granulated sugar**
2 teaspoons **salt**
1 cup **all-purpose flour**

Boil potatoes which have been peeled. Rice while still hot. Stir in the shortening, sugar, salt according to specifications. When cold stir in 1 cup flour for each 3 cups of potatoes. Take a piece of dough the size of a golf ball and roll it as thin as you possibly can and fry it on a large griddle. When lightly tan with brown blisters, turn and fry the other side. The griddle should be ungreased – and must be wiped off with a clean soft cloth from time to time to remove any flour. Fold the lefse in quarters and lay on a tea towel and cover with same.

NOTE: A ricer is a kitchen utensil which has a container at one end and is covered with small holes. When filled, the top is closed over it, and when the two handles are squeezed together, the contents come through string-like. We have a very old lefse rolling pin – not smooth like an ordinary rolling pin but with a finely grooved barrel.

LIMPA
Yield: 3 loaves

This is the best ever.

2 packages **dry yeast**
1/4 cup **warm water**
1 tablespoon **granulated sugar**
2 cups **warm water**
4 tablespoons **oil**
1/2 cup **molasses**
2 teaspoons grated **orange peel**
1 tablespoon **salt**
1 teaspoon **ground anise**
2 cups **rye flour**
4 - 5 cups **all-purpose flour**

Dissolve the yeast in the 1/4 cup water with the sugar. In a large bowl combine the 2 cups of water with oil, molasses, orange peel, salt and anise. Add yeast mixture and blend well. Add the rye flour and mix until smooth. Add enough all-purpose flour until it is easy to handle. Turn dough onto floured board and knead until smooth, about 10 minutes. Place in greased bowl and turn to coat. Cover and let rise in a warm place until double in bulk. Punch down and rise again. Form into 3 balls and place on well-greased cookie sheet. Cover loosely and let rise again. Preheat oven to 375 degrees and bake for 35 - 40 minutes.

MARINATED CUCUMBERS
Yield: 6 servings

Gurkasalad, in Norway, is always a standard on the smorgasbord table.

3 medium-sized **cucumbers**
1 tablespoon **salt**
2 tablespoons **sugar**
3/4 teaspoon **black pepper**
2 1/2 tablespoons **chopped parsley or dill**
1 tablespoon **water**
1 cup **wine vinegar**

Wash the cucumbers, pare them and slice them paper thin into a bowl. Sprinkle them with salt and mix. Press a plate over the cucumbers and let them stand about an hour. Drain the juice. Mix a dressing of the rest of the ingredients. Pour over the cucumbers and let stand 15 minutes or more.

ROSETTES
Yield: 3 - 4 dozen

Not very sweet but crisp and delicious, light and airy. Grandma's two rosette irons were like fine filigree.

2 **eggs**
1 tablespoon **sugar**
¼ teaspoon **salt**
1 cup **milk**
1 cup sifted **all-purpose flour**

Beat the eggs. Add all the other ingredients and mix well. Strain and let stand for an hour or so. Dip the rosette iron into hot grease and then wipe the iron with a soft cloth. Dip the iron immediately into the batter just up to the rim. Immerse immediately into hot grease. Cook for about 30 seconds – until nicely brown. They should drop off the iron! Just before serving, sift a little confectioners' sugar over them.

NOTE: If the rosette falls off the iron into the fat, there is too much grease on the iron. Wipe the iron a little more carefully. If the rosette doesn't come off easily when done, it means the iron is too hot. You'll catch on quickly!

SANDBAKKELS
Yield: 3 -4 dozen

A good Norwegian serves this delicacy at Christmas time – often times filled with lingonberries and topped with whipped cream. Or serve as is with a cup of good strong coffee

½ pound **butter** (it really must be butter)
1 cup **granulated sugar**
1 **egg**
1 teaspoon **almond or vanilla extract**
½ teaspoon **salt**
3 cups **all-purpose flour**

Preheat oven to 350 degrees. Thoroughly cream butter and sugar. Add egg and extract. Beat well. Cut in flour a little at a time. Mix gently. Press dough into the molds – as thin as possible. Bake for about 10 minutes. When they are beautifully brown remove from oven. After a minute or so gently squeeze the mold until the cookie is released. The cookie contracts a little as it cools.

NOTE: A hint from Grandma Everson: when pressing the dough into the molds, make it a little thinner in the bottom than on the sides because the heat causes some of the dough to slip down the sides of the mold. And you don't want a cookie with a bottom thicker than the sides. You remember the molds – little cup like tins with fluted sides!

YULEKAGE
Yield: 3 loaves

The best Norwegian Christmas Bread recipe I know – it came from the Home Economics instructor at Concordia College a lot of years ago!

2 packages **dry yeast** dissolved in ¼ cup **lukewarm water**
1 pint **milk**, scalded and cooled
1 cup **granulated sugar**
1 cup **butter or margarine**
1 teaspoon **salt**
1 teaspoon **cinnamon**
AT LEAST 1 TEASPOON **GROUND CARDAMOM** (Grandma Everson always put in at least twice that much!!)
2 **eggs**, beaten
approximately 7 cups of **all-purpose flour**, sifted
2 cups **golden raisins**
2 cups **mixed dried fruit** (citron, pineapple, cherries etc. – the kind one uses for fruitcake)

Dissolve yeast in lukewarm water. Scald and cool milk. Cream butter, sugar and salt. Add spices and slightly beaten eggs to the creamed mixture. When milk is lukewarm, add yeast and blend with butter, sugar and eggs. Add 3 cups of flour a little at a time and beat until smooth. Add the remaining flour and mix thoroughly. (At this point add as little or as much flour as needed to achieve a nice dough. It should not be sticky, but it should be soft.) Let dough rise in a warm place until it is double in size. Add fruit and punch down. Let it rise once again until it is double in size. Divide into three parts and shape into loaves (oblong or round) or braids. Place on greased pans and let rise again. Preheat oven to 350 degrees and bake for 40 to 60 minutes. It is done when it sounds hollow when tapped . Remove immediately from pans and place on wire racks to cool. If you like, you may frost them with a light glaze (1 cup Confectioners' sugar, 1 to 2 tablespoons milk and 1 teaspoon vanilla – "drizzling" consistency). Or you may choose to simply rub a little butter on the crust when it is removed from the oven. It gives it a nice shine and softens the crust somewhat.

Printed in the United States
19247LVS00006B/333